Critical Guides to French Te

GH00456885

6 Beckett: En attendant Godot *and* Fin de partie

Critical Guides to French Texts

EDITED BY ROGER LITTLE, WOLFGANG VAN EMDEN, DAVID WILLIAMS

BECKETT

En attendant Godot *and* Fin de partie

J. P. Little

*Lecturer in French,
St Patrick's College, Dublin*

Grant & Cutler Ltd
1981

I.S.B.N. 84-499-4974-2

DEPÓSITO LEGAL: V. 2.140 - 1981

Printed in Spain by
Artes Gráficas Soler, S. A. - Olivereta, 28 - Valencia (18)
for
GRANT AND CUTLER LTD
11 BUCKINGHAM STREET, LONDON, W.C.2.

Contents

For Roger

'Vivre est errer seul vivant
au fond d'un instant sans bornes'
(Malone meurt)

Prefatory Note

R EFERENCE is made to the editions of the texts published by
Editions de Minuit, Paris. For *En attendant Godot* the
1976 printing of the 1952 edition has, with one exception
which is noted, been used. The text of this later printing
contains certain textual revisions, notably excisions, and has
different pagination. For *Fin de partie* I have used the 1957
edition. English translations by Beckett himself are readily
available, published by Faber. Italicised numbers in parenthe-
ses, followed by page references, refer to the numbered items in
the select bibliography at the end of this volume.

I wish to acknowledge the cooperation of the Librarian
and staff of the Manuscript Room, Trinity College, Dublin,
for facilitating access to unpublished material. My thanks are
also due to several colleagues and friends for discussion of
points of detail, and especially to my husband, whose creative
support and critical eye have proved invaluable.

Dún Laoghaire   J. P. L.

1

Impact, genesis

'nothing to express, nothing
from which to express, nothing
with which to express, no
power to express, no desire
to express, together with the
obligation to express'
(Dialogues with Georges Duthuit)

SINCE its first production in 1953, *En attendant Godot,*
Beckett's first play to be published and staged, has
probably generated more critical heat than any other modern
play. It has been produced in thousands of theatres, great and
small, in all parts of the world, in any number of interpretations and settings, dissected, argued over, reviled, hailed as
opening a new era in Western drama — it has been subject to
every possible fate except that of being ignored. The production in 1957 of Beckett's next play, *Fin de partie,* did nothing
to still the critical controversy surrounding him, and he, char-
acteristically, replied to the storm he had created by retreating
further and further from the limelight. His reported comment
that he often thanked heaven at not being a critic about to
write a book about Beckett (*25,* p. 4) does nothing to allay a
prospective critic's nervousness at adding yet another grain to
the massive and well-nigh impossible heap of Beckett scholar-
ship.

It is difficult however at this distance in time to recreate
the impact of those early productions and realise the sense of
newness and frequently of scandal which the play aroused, so
fully has it become absorbed into the theatre of our times.
Almost everything recognisably 'modern' owes a debt to

Godot: Arrabal, Stoppard, Albee, Pinter, to mention only some of the best-known, are, in Martin Esslin's words, all 'children of Godot' (*25,* p. 12). The sense of the play being a landmark, conveyed by William Saroyan when he said that *Godot* would 'make it easier for me and everyone else to write freely in the theatre' (*25,* pp. 11-12), is precisely what makes us accept it now as the norm.

The fact that *Godot* was put on at all is owed to a happy accident — but a significantly theatrical one. Roger Blin, who first agreed to stage the play, and whose enthusiasm was crucial in Beckett's eventual success as a dramatic writer, would have preferred to stage the still unpublished and unplayed *Eleuthéria,* a safer bet from some points of view since it was more obviously traditional, and also had women's roles. But *Eleuthéria* is on a grand scale, necessitating many actors and elaborate stage settings, and Blin could not afford such a production, so he settled for *Godot.* After a great deal of difficulty in finding a suitable theatre prepared to take on such an apparently risky venture, J.-M. Serreau at the little Théâtre de Babylone agreed to stage the play, and *Godot* opened on 5 January 1953.

The French critics were on the whole perceptive and some quite enthusiastic. Sylvain Zegel in *Libération* (7.i.53) was among these, as was Jacques Lemarchand in *Le Figaro Litté-raire* (17.i.53), who saw unusual qualities in the play. It was Anouilh a little later in *Arts-Spectacles* (27.ii-5.iii.53) who coined the definition which was to become famous: 'le sketch des "Pensées de Pascal" par les Fratellini'. He recognised the importance of the production as being on a par with the opening of Pirandello in Paris in 1923.

In August 1955 the English version opened at the Arts Theatre Club in London. Harold Hobson and Kenneth Tynan, the most influential of the London theatre critics, were both enthusiastic, although Tynan began his review defensively (*Observer,* 7.viii.55). But reaction was by no means universally favourable: the views of a certain section of the theatre-going public were illustrated by the judgement of Marya Mannes, who saw the play as 'typical of the self-delusion of which certain intellectuals are capable, embracing obscurity, pretense, ugliness, and negation as protective colouring for their own confusions' (*24*, p. 9). Harsh words for a work that was destined to change the nature of Western theatre!

Reaction to Alan Schneider's initial American production, at the Coconut Grove Playhouse, Miami, in January 1956, was largely uncomprehending, with a fair part of the audience leaving after the first act. When the play opened in New York in April, critics tended to be puzzled, evasive, or searching for a meaning which eluded them. Walter Kerr for instance in the *New York Herald Tribune* (29 April) described it as a 'cerebral tennis match' that 'can be read variously and furiously as Christian, existentialist or merely stoic allegory' (*24*, p. 10), while Henry Hewes in the *Saturday Review* produced one of the early extravaganzas in Beckett interpretation, claiming that Godot was God, Pozzo the Capitalist-Aristocrat, Lucky Labor-Proletariat, and Mr Albert just possibly Schweitzer of that name (*24*, p. 11). The allegorical approach was also adopted by G. S. Fraser in February of that year, in an article in the *Times Literary Supplement* which sparked off a long correspondence on the play, when he asserted that Beckett had written 'a modern morality play on permanent Christian themes.' His religious interpretation made Vladimir and Estragon stand for the contemplative life, while Beckett's fundamental message was one of religious consolation. Beckett himself has since tried to fight his way through the dense jungle of early criticism, stressing that 'the early success of *Waiting for Godot* was based on a fundamental misunderstanding, critics and public alike insisted on interpreting in allegorical or symbolic terms a play which was striving all the time to avoid definition' (*24*, p. 10).

If reaction to *Godot* was mixed, *Fin de partie* fared even worse. Blin, enthusiastic about the play, was unable to find a theatre in Paris prepared to take it, and the original Paris production had to be cancelled. The first performance therefore took place in London, in French, at the Royal Court Theatre. Because of the language barrier, there were few early notices. Harold Hobson's was the most positive, calling the play 'a magnificent theatrical experience' (*Sunday Times,* 7.iv.57). But Tynan did not repeat his enthusiasm for the earlier play, saying that *Fin de partie* 'piled on the agony until I thought my skull would split' (*Observer,* 7.iv.57). Beckett himself did not much like the atmosphere at the Royal Court, which he found too large and oppressive. The production he said was 'rather grim, like playing to mahogany, or rather teak' (*16,* p. 185). When the play finally went to Paris, to the Studio des Champs-Elysées, in April 1957, he found the atmosphere much more appropriate. There, he said, 'the hooks went in ...'. But critical reaction was equally divided: Marc Bernard in *Les Nouvelles Littéraires* (9.v.57) gave it an allegorical reading (Hamm being the Intellectual and Clov the Common Man) and expressed the view that the whole play was the product of a particularly nasty form of masochism. Jacques Lemarchand in *Le Figaro Littéraire* for 11 May 1957 spoke of the play's universality and greatness, while Gabriel Marcel said that it was responsible for one of the most painful evenings he had ever spent in the theatre, and Jean-Jacques Gautier, predictably, claimed: 'c'est laid, c'est sale, c'est désolant, c'est malsain, c'est vide et misérable' (*Le Figaro,* 3.v.57). After Schneider's 1959 production at the Cherry Lane Theatre, New York, Walter Kerr spoke of the 'aura of smugness that always hovers around a private language, the defiant treadmill of directionless conversation, the knowledge that the author is deliberately playing blind-man's buff, the emotional aridity of a world without a face' (*Herald Tribune,* 29.i.58), while Brooks Atkinson in the *New York Times* (29.i.58), although praising the overall impression, confessed he found the dialogue often baffling.

With such critical reaction it is not surprising that Beckett has tended to withdraw from the fray and retreat to his 'hole in the Marne mud' (*16,* p. 183). But the sense of newness and of shock, whether expressed positively or negatively, which greeted Beckett's early dramatic writing, should not be allowed to obscure the fact that these works did not emerge fully clad and without precedent from their author's head. Beckett's international reputation was established through the theatre, but by 1953 when *Godot* was first produced, he had a considerable volume of writing behind him, some published, some not, none of which had attracted the same quality or quantity of attention, but where frequent echoes can be found of the themes and even the writing of the later drama. This is not to imply, obviously, that Beckett was simply re-working himself; but Beckett is one of the most consistent of writers, and has tended to explore the same problems over and over again with remarkable tenacity. His search is above all one of form, and through this search — to 'find a form that accommodates the mess' (*18*, p. 523) — the same preoccupations are revealed.

That he was preoccupied with these questions even before his major effort as a creative writer began is illustrated by the essay on Proust, written in 1929 as a young graduate in Paris. Although this essay is ostensibly a study of the French novelist, it contains in fact some highly personal reflections on the question of time, which no account of the origin of the various themes in *Godot* and other works can afford to ignore. What we have here in essence is a prose statement, in language which is frequently striking though sometimes over-elaborate and self-conscious, of the major preoccupations of the later play. The moments of consciousness which Vladimir and Estragon spend their time trying to ward off by their endless rituals and time-filling exercises, for example, are here said to

> represent the perilous zones in the life of the individual, dangerous, precarious, painful, mysterious and fertile, when for a moment the boredom of living is replaced by the suffering of being (*10*, p. 19).

The tension here expressed in language is lived and represented in immediate terms by Vladimir and Estragon, articulated by their very presence on the stage and the anguish which they communicate. The form has changed: the problem remains constant.

I shall return to this question of form in a later chapter. For the moment it may be of some interest to mention the work that most closely pre-figures *Godot,* since the development from one to the other illustrates clearly this concern with

finding the most appropriate form for what Beckett was trying
to say. I am referring to the early novel *Mercier et Camier,*
which Beckett still dislikes, and whose publication he allowed
only relatively recently. [1] The novel, like the play, has as its
central characters two tramp-like figures whose wanderings,
separations and reunions form the main theme. But the novel,
with its narrative requirements, has the possibility of actually
following these wanderings, giving a looseness of structure in
sharp contrast with the play, whose dramatic limitations — the
necessity for the actors to be seen on stage at all times — bring
into sharp focus the simple fact of the characters' existence,
their 'being there'. The form itself has imposed conditions on
the material, which has resulted in a tightening-up and a sim-
plification of the original themes, giving a stark dramatic unity
to the whole.

Another illustration of the primacy of the question of form
when considering the two works can be seen in a passage from
the novel where the narrator is considering the means of communication between Mercier and Camier:

> S'ensuivit un long débat, entrecoupé de longs silences,
> pendant lesquels la méditation s'effectuait. Il arrivait
> alors, tantôt à Mercier, tantôt à Camier, de s'abîmer si
> avant dans ses pensées que la voix de l'autre, reprenant
> son argumentation, était impuissante à l'en tirer, ou ne
> se faisait pas entendre. Ou, arrivés simultanément à des
> conclusions souvent contraires, ils se mettaient simulta-
> nément à les exprimer. Il n'était pas rare non plus que
> l'un tombât en syncope avant que l'autre eût achevé son
> exposé. Et de temps en temps ils se regardaient, incapa-
> bles de prononcer un mot, l'esprit vide (*9,* pp. 22-3).

And towards the end of the novel, the narrator comments:
'Ils se parleront encore, mais ce sera par l'effet du hasard,
comme on dit. Mais se sont-ils jamais parlé autrement?'

---

[1] A full discussion of the development from *Mercier et Camier,*
and of the genesis of *Godot* in general, can be found in the Introduc-
tion to Duckworth's edition of the play (see bibliography, item *2*).

(p. 155). What better statement could there be of the permanent failure of Vladimir and Estragon in their attempts to
communicate? But the difference is that in the play there is
no narrator to spell it out for us, the whole process gains in
immediacy by being presented to us dramatically, and we the
audience assist in the creation of this failure.

There are many other parallels between the two works.
Both couples greet each other with a joyful embrace when
meeting again in the morning — but both reflect that they
might be better off going their separate ways. Whereas Vladimir and Estragon wait for Godot and are not sure of the
meeting-place, Camier misses a rendez-vous with a Monsieur
Conaire, who was going to take up some sort of business
partnership with them. A tree figures prominently in both
works: the single tree of *Godot* is paralleled by the beech-tree
in the Square Saint-Ruth in *Mercier et Camier,* which assumes
a certain importance. There is a basic similarity in setting,
much of *Mercier et Camier* taking place on the *haute lande*
outside a city, parallel to the plateau on which *Godot* takes
place. In both works there is a certain nostalgia for a time when
they were warm and dry — but what tramp would not indulge
in this periodically? — and an agreement not to tell each other
their dreams. Interestingly, too, the enigmatic passage in *Godot*
where Vladimir muses on the fact that 'Moi aussi, un autre
me regarde...' (p. 128) is mirrored by Mercier when he says
'C'est drôle, j'ai souvent l'impression que nous ne sommes
pas seuls [...]. Comme la présence d'un tiers... Elle nous en-
veloppe' (p. 146). But these very real parallels take place
within a formal structure that differs radically between the two
works. The success of *Godot* depends very largely on Beckett
having found the right way of stating what he wanted to say —
or, since in his view 'to be an artist is to fail' (*10,* p. 125), the
approximation that best illustrates the object aimed at and
that failure.

Such changes as there are between the original manuscript
of *Godot* and the final published version also reflect Beckett's
preoccupation with form, in so far as they show him grappling
with an unfamiliar dramatic medium. The play was written

quickly — according to Colin Duckworth the first page of the manuscript bears the date '9 October 1948' and the last '29 January 1949' (*2*, p. xlv) — and many features which appear for instance in the final English version are due to trial and error in rehearsal and performance, with Beckett and Blin together realising what worked and what didn't. For example the fact that the tree in the English version has 'four or five leaves' at the beginning of Act II, whereas the French is 'couvert de feuilles' is due apparently to their realisation that it would be theatrically more effective thus. Sometimes changes relate to Beckett's desire not to be over-explicit in a medium which had a multiplicity of ways for suggesting meaning. For instance, the play was originally to be performed in the round, but Beckett felt that this made the circularity theme too obvious, and preferred a less direct statement of it (*18*, p. 421). In the original version, too, the boy actually brings a letter from Godot, but Beckett suppressed this as he felt it made the presence of Godot too physically explicit. A letter after all implies a writer. Overall then, such changes as were made developed from the experience gained through performance, and much of this work was done in rehearsal or even subsequently.

Fin de partie was in this respect different, in that it went through several stages in manuscript before emerging as the play we know. Beckett originally conceived it as a two-acter, and when he wrote to Alan Schneider on 12 April 1956, telling him he was working on a new play, it was obviously giving him a certain amount of trouble. 'It has turned out a three-legged giraffe, to mention only the architectonics, and leaves me in doubt whether to take a leg off or add one on' (*16*, p. 183). The fact that the leg was removed in the end is an indication of Beckett's sureness of feeling for form, since the single act conveys by its very nature the gradual disintegration which is at the heart of the play. But before this stage was reached, there were two successive full-length, two-act versions, and it is one of Beckett's most consciously worked creations. The most significant changes between the early two-act version and the final play concern a radical pruning and condensation of what Beckett was wanting to express. [2] The early version contains a good deal of stage 'business' with ladders, alarm clocks, telescopes, pain-killers, insecticides etc., which is reduced to a minimum or to a mere suggestion in the final version. There is also a certain amount of explicit violence: Hamm gives Nagg a series of 'coups sur le crâne' while he is pilloried and unable to retreat into his dustbin. The final version gains in menace from this physical violence becoming verbal and implicit rather than being crudely spelled-out. By comparison with the stripped economy of the final version the early draft is cluttered and over-specific. There are also features which Beckett clearly felt did not work: for instance, when Hamm, inspired by a desire to procreate, wants a woman, Clov re-enters dressed as one, then seeing the child outside, leaves the stage and comes back as a child. The Biblical allusions, restrained in the final version, are made much of, and there is a long passage where Clov reads the story of Noah and the flood, and tells of the families of Shem. Many things which are simply hinted at in the final version are spelled out in the early one: for example, Nell dies at the end of Act I, and her dustbin is removed in Act II. Throughout, there is a move from the specific to the merely suggestive, and from a certain over-emphasis to a more elliptic and condensed style. A few examples will serve to illustrate the way in which Beckett tightened up the writing stylistically. In the original Act II, 'B' (Clov) says 'Je vais te laisser', and 'A' (Hamm) replies 'Tu me laisseras quand je te dirai de me laisser'. [3] In the final version this becomes

> Clov — Je te quitte.
> Hamm — Non!

---

[2] For an analysis of the successive versions, see Ruby Cohn, 'The beginning of *Endgame*', in *27*, pp. 319-23. See also *5*, pp. 6-11, and *18*, pp. 447-464.

[3] MS of early version of *Fin de partie* held in the Library of Trinity College, Dublin.

A's 'Nous sommes arrivés déjà?' becomes: Hamm — Déjà?
Sometimes a passage is expanded slightly, to give it a more
forceful violence. For instance A's 'Eh bien, continue', when
trying to get B to enquire further about the progress of his
'story', becomes 'Mais pousse plus loin, bon sang, pousse plus
loin!'.

Apart from these early versions of the play itself, there is
evidence that even before the play began to take shape in two
acts, Beckett was working over some of the themes that were to
appear in the finished work. For example, Richard L. Admussen
has recently brought to light an abandoned draft of some nine
pages, dating from before 1955, possibly several years earlier,
which recalls several of the features of Beckett's later dramatic
work. There are two characters, Ernest, 'renversé sur sa croix',
attended by his wife, Alice, who serves him in much the same
way as Clov does Hamm. There is a similar play with
ladders — Alice has to climb one to minister to Ernest's
needs — there is the familiar 'running out' of various requirements (e.g. the aperitif), and Alice's inexplicable remaining
with Ernest when all attachment has vanished. (Here however
Alice is prepared to recite Ernest's 'qualités' as a reason for
remaining with him.) There are visual similarities too — at the
beginning Ernest's face is covered with a handkerchief, and the
setting is the same rather indeterminate 'intérieur'.

In another abandoned dramatic work quoted by Admussen,
'Mime du rêveur A', there is an echo of *Fin de partie* in the
single character 'A', who steps on a stool to look out of the
window, and gives himself three sleep-inducing injections. He
also moves his rocking-chair to different positions in the room
(the rocking-chair recalls also of course Murphy).

There is therefore a fair amount of evidence that Beckett
was working over the various themes of *Fin de partie* long
before it took shape as the play we know. There are also a
good number of parallels to episodes in the play in his published work. *L'Innommable* provides several interesting examples in this respect. There is of course the whole business of
story-telling, though this is by no means confined to these two
works. The narrator's purpose in story-telling in *L'Innommable*

can in fact help to explain certain aspects of Hamm's narrative urge in *Fin de partie,* since things are spelled out in the novel which are only implicit in the play. For instance, the narrator admits that his stories are invented to put off the hour when he must speak of himself, since only by speaking of himself will he be able one day to end (7, p. 28). Hamm's reluctance to finish ('il est temps que cela finisse et cependant j'hésite encore à — [...] — finir' [p. 17]) can be seen in this light, providing one of the poles of the tension underlying the whole play, between ending and infinite duration. Much of this tension, together with an evocation of the actual setting of *Fin de partie,* is contained in the following lines from *L'Innomma-ble,* where the narrator speaks of being in the same place as always, perhaps merely

> l'intérieur de mon crâne lointain, où autrefois j'errais [...] toujours murmurant mes vieilles histoires, ma vieille histoire [...]. Cependant j'ai peur, peur de ce que mes mots vont faire de moi, de ma cachette, encore une fois (7, p. 26).

The narrator is also, like Clov, convinced that he has no words with which to express what he wants to say except the words of others, no vehicle which would fit exactly the chaotic universe to be expressed, and conveys his anguish at having to speak, in a borrowed language, of things that don't concern him (7, pp. 62-3). I shall return to this point later in this study when I examine in more detail the whole crucial question of language. For the present it is sufficient to emphasise its centrality in Beckett's creative process.

There are other features of the play, some of them major ones, that originally crop up in the novels. The heap-of-time theme for instance occurs twice in *L'Innommable* (pp. 171, 181), where again its somewhat expanded form helps to explain its rather cryptic use in the play. The general theme of the guilt implicit in the mere fact of existence, and of life itself being a kind of penance for the fact of being born — an idea expressed for example by Estragon in *Godot* (p. 13) — is common to much of Beckett's writing, and is given typical

expression in *Malone meurt,* where the narrator reflects on
the identity of Macmann, but concludes that it doesn't matter
in fact: 'Du moment que c'est encore ce qu'on appelle un
vivant il n'y a pas à se tromper, c'est le coupable' (pp. 161-2).

One could easily multiply examples of echoes in both plays
from a large number of Beckett's earlier works. All would be
revealing of the continuity of Beckett's preoccupations throughout his writing, and of how his increasing concern with formal
problems has led to a high degree of concentration of ideas
which were given more explicit treatment in earlier works.
But I trust I have given sufficient examples to illustrate this
point, and to show that, however new the formal expression
of *En attendant Godot* and *Fin de partie,* their themes were
already present in Beckett's earlier work.

Moving outwards from Beckett's own writing, mention
could also be made here of various 'influences' which Beckett
came under at different points in his life, through his contacts
or his reading or both, and which had a more or less profound
effect on his writing. One could consider at length for example
the relationship between Beckett and Joyce, who without
doubt exercised a deep influence on the young Beckett during
their association in Paris, but it was an influence that had
more or less worked itself out by the time Beckett turned to
the drama, a form alien in any case to Joyce's vision. In terms
of his 'Irishness', much could no doubt be made of the debt
he owes to earlier Irish writers, particularly the satirists such
as Swift, which whom he has much in common — though here
again the relationship is much clearer in the novels than in the
plays. The peculiarly Irish combination of the Jesuit and the
Puritan is at the root of much of his humour, which functions
as a kind of escape mechanism from over-seriousness. Faced
with fundamental problems recognised as insoluble, Beckett,
like other Irish writers such as Joyce and Flann O'Brien, reacts
with an almost embarrassed humour, a jokiness which reflects
the impossibility of confronting such matters in total seriousness.

Certain other parallels and 'influences' will be dealt with
in the course of this study: Beckett's attraction to the post-
Cartesian philosopher Geulincx is of some importance in a

consideration of the mind-body split which can be traced in so much of Beckett's writing, and will be considered in Chapter 3. Beckett's debt to Dante deserves a study on its own, but Dante's name will crop up from time to time in the following pages, by no means to exhaust the subject, but to give pointers to the reader who may thus be helped to set Beckett's work in a more general literary and cultural context. But the whole question of 'influences' is a very thorny one, and needs very careful handling. Beckett, like many writers, tends to dismiss suggestions of influence, and probably rightly so: no writing of genius can be split down into its supposed component parts, influence from such and such a writer here, echoes of a past experience there, and to attempt such an analysis is to do a profound injustice to the work as a whole. Beckett's writing in its newness is entirely his own, a deeply personal vision that draws inevitably on the literature of the past, but which in its final synthesis is totally his.

There is an area in which the question of sources can be fruitful, however, and that is the whole tradition of Western theatre into which Beckett's plays fit. Their newness does not preclude their being firmly rooted in certain aspects of theatrical tradition, and it is to these that I want to turn in the next chapter.

2
Play

'Ici est mon seul ailleurs'
(L'Innommable)

J ust as Beckett's plays have their origins in his creative effort in general, being present embryonically in much of his earlier work, so in spite of their newness they reach out to a long and very central theatrical tradition. Beckett had been interested in theatre from his student days, and in particular popular theatre. As a student in Dublin he frequented not only the Gate theatre, where he saw European theatrical experimentation at work — Pirandello and so forth — but also the Queen's, which produced melodrama, vaudeville, slapstick (*18*, p. 48). He also followed the cinema closely, developing a passion for such comic giants as Laurel and Hardy, and Chaplin. This interest in the non-literary theatre, the theatre of gesture and situation as opposed to that of discursive dialogue, is clearly brought out in both *Godot* and *Fin de partie*. Take the two main characters in *Godot* for example. As Geneviève Serreau points out, it is too restricting to call them tramps, since this fixes them in a given social situation, places them in a context in which they belong only partially — they clearly *do* have elements of the tramp about them, from their ragged clothes and hand-to-mouth existence to Vladimir's search for lice in his hat. But what they recall much more closely is a pair of music-hall comics, or traditional clowns or their modern equivalents such as the Marx brothers, by their independence of any precise social setting and their universality. As in the traditional form, the notion of couple is indispensable: the action and the dialogue move forward only through the constant friction of one element on another, and traditionally this is made possible by the temperamental differences between the two. Although these differences are somewhat attenuated in Didi and Gogo, they exist sufficiently for a kind of parody of the traditional comic situation to take place. Instead of the constant polished patter of the traditional pair, what we are presented with in *Godot* are short spurts of inspiration, where the dialogue bounces briskly backwards and forwards, followed by a sudden fizzling out when the void underlying their situation again becomes apparent. The parody of clown-language in this way becomes a parody of the human situation itself. Estragon's inability to remember what has happened the day before, which provides the material for many of the friends' exchanges, becomes not merely a comic lapse, but a source of metaphysical anguish to Vladimir in his attempt to situate himself in time and space.

If the cross-talk of Vladimir and Estragon recalls the music-hall pair, the physical slapstick used by Beckett harks back to the tradition of the *commedia dell'arte* as much as anything else. [1] The *lazzi,* or stage business, used by the *commedia dell'arte* as interludes between passages of dialogue, are taken up by Beckett but frequently wrested from their original comic context by being given a kind of metaphysical significance. This is not to say that the comic element disappears: it is simply that in all Beckett's writing the apparently most innocent words and actions have cracks in them revealing a nothingness that terrifies through the laughter. So for instance in Act II of *Godot,* where all four characters fall and finish in an absurd heap on stage, audience reaction does not remain at the level of laughter: their sudden horizontality becomes a stage in the process of total disintegration which can only provoke an uneasy response. Even the hat routine in the second act, an apparently innocent enough piece of slapstick, derived it would seem from Beckett's memories of the Marx brothers' *Duck Soup,* has a kind of disturbing quality about it in its

---

[1] On *Godot* and the tradition of the *commedia dell'arte,* see among others Edith Kern, 'Beckett and the spirit of the *commedia dell'arte',* *27,* pp. 260ff.

suggestion of endlessness. Like all the other episodes, it fizzles out in pointlessness and frustration: Vladimir having decided upon Lucky's hat wants to 'play at' Lucky and Pozzo, but Estragon cannot remember anything of their passing the previous day, and is an unhelpful partner in the game (p. 102). 'Connais pas' is his only response.

There are clear hints too of the circus. As I mentioned in the previous chapter, Blin had at first wanted to stage the play as a circus, but decided with Beckett that this was too restricting. But the suggestion of the circus is made and insisted upon when the two characters comment on the 'charmante soirée' they are having, being 'entertained' by Pozzo and Lucky.

> Vladimir — On se croirait au spectacle.
> Estragon — Au cirque.
> Vladimir — Au music-hall.
> Estragon — Au cirque.   (pp. 47-48)

And indeed Pozzo and Lucky do recall circus characters, Pozzo the ring-master with his whip and his air of cruel menace, Lucky the cowed animal who responds mechanically because he has no alternative. Because Lucky is still physically recognisably human, the result is not pure circus, but a kind of cruel parody of circus. But the conscious theatricality of circus, and its mechanical, fixed quality, make it a much more appropriate image than the purely human one of the master-slave relationship, which is essentially psychologically based. By reducing the Pozzo-Lucky relationship to its mechanical essentials Beckett has gone beyond psychology into a far more horrifying realm, at the same time preserving in a kind of grotesque pathos the tattered remains of a human situation.

The self-consciousness implicit in this kind of theatre is apparent throughout both plays, and again harks back to an immediate, popular tradition, as opposed to the more 'literary' model derived from Aristotle's concept of theatre as an imitation of life. In *Godot* there are frequent reminders that the play is a play: when Estragon tries to escape through the backcloth, for example, Vladimir comments 'Imbécile! Il n'y a pas d'issue par là', and directs him towards the auditorium: 'Là il n'y a personne. Sauve-toi par là' (p. 104). And when Vladimir leaves the stage, presumably to urinate, Estragon points the way — 'Au fond du couloir, à gauche'. 'Garde ma place', says Vladimir (p. 48). In *Fin de partie* the self-consciousness is related rather to the question of play and of story-telling. Hamm's opening lines, 'A [...] moi. [...] De jouer', gives a clear indication of the play-element, here referring to the chess-game that is one of the play's central images. His repeated comment 'Ça avance', creates the same impression of standing outside his situation, watching his own progress from the exterior. As Clov goes out for the last time he comments 'C'est ce que nous appelons gagner la sortie' (p. 109) — but the theatrical reference, far from underlining the reality of the situation, creates an air of uncertainty. There is no finality in the theatre: tonight's exit is repeated tomorrow, and the next day; death itself is no escape, since in the theatre dying is only one action among many that are repeated an indeterminate number of times.

The chess-image is of obvious importance in *Fin de partie,* one of the principal ways in which Beckett conveys the idea of self-observation in this play. The chess-player is involved in a game, the rules of which are not of his making, and which he operates from the outside, being conscious of his own moves as he plays. The title of the play is clearly significant: Deirdre Bair recounts that when Beckett told some English-speaking friends that he was writing a play called *Fin de partie* they translated it *End of the game.* No, he objected, it's *Endgame,* as in chess (*18,* p. 467). Beckett has a long-standing interest in chess: it is for example a notable feature in the early novel *Murphy,* whose hero, employed in the local mental institution, plays day-long games of chess with one of the inmates, Mr Endon, a gentle, languorous schizophrenic. Beckett was a friend of Marcel Duchamp, a great chess-player, who frequented cafés in Paris where chess-players gathered, and wrote an occasional chess-column for *Ce Soir* which Beckett apparently followed (*18,* p. 465). He was also co-author of a book on chess, *Opposition and Sister Squares Are Reconciled,*

dealing specifically with the endgame, which Beckett knew
well. In brief, the endgame is the third and last part of the
game of chess. In the first part, the pieces are brought out and
strategies begun, which are then developed in the second part,
or middle game, where moves are organised. In the third
part, or endgame, depending on one's previous position, either
the advantage is consolidated into an outright win, or there
is an attempt to cancel out the disadvantage incurred in the
middle game. The essential feature from the point of view of
the play is that by this time the moves open to both kings are
strictly limited. The kings are free to come to the centre of
the board and confront each other, but there is little they can
do to alter the situation.

The identification of Hamm with the chess-king is made
clear in Beckett's comments to the Berlin Hamm when he
was assisting in the direction of that production. His comments
are interesting in that they emphasise one of the poles of the
play, Hamm's reluctance to end, his desire to put off the end
and continue in the known.

> Hamm is a king in this chess game lost from the start.
> From the start he knows he is making loud senseless
> moves. That he will make no progress at all with the
> gaff. Now at the last he makes a few senseless moves
> as only a bad player would. A good one would have
> given up long ago. He is only trying to delay the inevit-
> able end. Each of his gestures is one of the last useless
> moves which put off the end. He is a bad player (22,
> p. 152).

Hamm's own consciousness of his situation is underlined here
by Beckett. *He knows* he will lose this game, which was not of
his making and which he did not choose to play. He plays
because he has no alternative, making a few last bad moves
as his only possible protest against the situation in which he
finds himself. He is player but also chess-piece, and this is
reflected in the play in the way he orders Clov to move him
around the stage, whose image is the chess-board. Like the
chess-piece, he cannot move himself, but he is nevertheless

the king who commands — an interesting comment perhaps on the way in which even the chess-image is parodied. This is no straight game of chess, but a parallel parody, which by virtue of its dislocation has lost its quality of pure game and become something much more sinister. The game of chess is undermined, parodied, while at the same time parodying life itself. Clov extends the chess-parody, as he is both pawn — his capacity as servant to Hamm makes him totally dependent on his master's commands, having little freedom of independent action — and player, since Hamm depends on him for physical movement. He is also possibly regarded as a knight at one point, where Hamm refers to his going round to visit 'mes pauvres' — and Clov points out that he sometimes went on horseback (p. 22).

The notion of the player who stands back and watches himself playing is echoed, especially in *Fin de partie,* by that of the self-conscious story-teller. Story-telling occurs again and again in Beckett's work, and the relationship between the teller and the story is always a very complex one. Sometimes the result is essentially autobiographical, as in *La Dernière Bande,* where Krapp listens to his own version of his previous self — but even here the story told is deliberately contrived and dramatised for the purpose of the recording. The ultimate urge in the story-telling of Beckett's characters does not in fact seem to be an autobiographical one, and this must be taken into account when interpreting Hamm's 'story'. Although it is obviously tempting to identify the boy who, we suppose, [2] arrived at the narrator's door with his father one Christmas, with Clov, the relationship is clearly not so straightforward. A comment by the narrator of *L'Innommable* is revealing here, when he speaks of the madness 'd'avoir à parler et de ne le pouvoir, sauf de choses qui ne me regardent pas, qui ne comptent pas, auxquelles je ne crois pas, dont ils m'ont gavé pour m'empêcher de dire qui je suis' (7, pp. 62-3). The dis-

---

[2] In fact this is never made clear by Beckett; all we are told is that the father arrived, and after a lot of argument the narrator possibly agreed to receive the son too.

tanciation here is complete: while giving the impression at
times that he is recounting real events from his own past, he
makes it clear that not only are these events not 'true' in any
autobiographical sense, but that they are a hindrance on the
path to the only knowledge that counts, knowledge of the Self.
So Hamm tells his story, and like the game of chess, it both
fills out the endlessness of time with makeshift action, conveying
a spurious reality to what has none, and prevents him from
ending, from arriving at the point of death which would reveal
to him the sum of his life. Far from being autobiographical,
the ultimate aim in this story-telling seems to be to say nothing.
Words, in so far as they relate to the everyday world, chain
one to that world. L'Innommable reproaches 'cette voix [...]
qui ne rime à rien, qui empêche d'être rien' (7, p. 140), and
elsewhere confesses his need to speak and say nothing, while
regretting the fact that whatever you say, a little meaning
always creeps in (7, p. 27). So Hamm exclaims in horror 'On
n'est pas en train de ... de ... signifier quelque chose?' (p. 49).
Meaning to their existence would only put off the longed-for
day beyond meaning when the babble of illusory voices will
be stilled and the ultimate reality of nothingness revealed.

    Story-telling is frequently associated with a generalised
metaphysical guilt, illustrated in *Godot* (p. 13) when Vladimir asks 'Si on se repentait?' Estragon — De quoi? Vladimir — Eh bien... *(Il cherche.)* On n'aurait pas besoin d'en-
trer dans les détails. Estragon — D'être né? — the one 'crime'
for which in rational terms they cannot be held responsable,
but the one that engenders all the others. Story-telling is seen
by l'Innommable to be a kind of penance for this sin, and his
ultimate right to fall silent is dependent on its fulfilment: 'J'ai
un pensum à faire, avant d'être libre, [...] libre de me taire, de
ne plus écouter [...]. On m'a donné un pensum, à ma naissance
peut-être, pour me punir d'être né peut-être...' (7, p. 39).
Hamm's story is full of guilt-feelings about 'tous ceux que
j'aurais pu aider', he defends himself feebly against Clov's
accusation that he let la Mère Pegg 'die of darkness' when she
wanted oil for her lamp, and brushes off his cruelty to the old
man who wanted food for his child by relating it to a much

more fundamental cruelty, that of being in the world at all. And yet we know that even this guilt is a sham: as l'Innommable points out, 'Les regrets, ça vous avance, ça vous rapproche de la fin du monde' (*7*, p. 140), it is merely a device in the pursuit of the end. And the very act of story-telling, the theatrically self-conscious relating of events that have no necessary connection with one's own past, is a means of hiding from oneself the fundamental guilt involved in existence itself. Hamm as narrator constantly transfers the responsibility for his actions onto another, and his inability to accept his own sufferings makes him inflict suffering on another. Humankind cannot bear too much reality, and one of the obvious 'ways out' is to create literature out of one's situation. When that fails, there is the reaction of the sadist.

Beckett in fact has portrayed suffering in a way few modern writers have equalled: not the suffering that ennobles, or that evokes pity in others, but suffering as it really is, 'le malheur', as Simone Weil called it, affliction so acute and so pointless that it degrades, destroys a person's humanity, and to which the only possible reaction on the part of the sufferer is to lash out like a wounded animal against the nearest victim. So Hamm's treatment of his parents is a reflection, not so much of his feelings for them, but of his despairing rage at the human condition of which he is a part. The very theatricality of the language in which he expresses his suffering underlines its intensity, by indicating that he cannot talk about it on a personal level. At the beginning of the play, having first cleared his throat and prepared himself for his stage appearance, he asks

> Peut-il y a- *(bâillements)* — y avoir misère plus ... plus haute que la mienne? Sans doute. Autrefois. Mais aujourd'hui? *(Un temps.)* Mon père? *(Un temps.)* Ma mère? *(Un temps.)* Mon chien? *(Un temps.)* Oh je veux bien qu'ils souffrent autant que de tels êtres peuvent souffrir. Mais est-ce dire que nos souffrances se valent? Sans doute. *(Un temps.)* Non, tout est a- *(bâillements)* -bsolu,

(fier) plus on est grand et plus on est plein. *(Un temps. Morne.)* Et plus on est vide. [3]

The alternate movement of theatrical declamation and immediate undermining of what has just been said stresses both the desire to escape from an intolerable situation by adopting an alternative persona, and the realisation that such an escape is impossible.

The same combination of contrived theatricality to protect against the intolerable, and sadistic cruelty towards those closest to him is to be found of course in Pozzo. The chess-king lording it over the board gives way to the ring-master cracking his whip at his subservient performers, but the motivation is the same. Pozzo does not have the same urge to tell stories as Hamm, but has a constant need to dramatise the void of his own existence, specialising in elaborate and vacuous reasoning, as when for instance he tries to explain why Lucky doesn't put his bags down (p. 41). Before commencing his 'act' he makes sure everyone is listening and, not content with merely clearing his throat, takes out a little vaporiser. After his 'purple passage' on the setting of the sun and the coming of night (p. 52), he sheds his role as narrator and is anxious to know how Vladimir and Estragon have found his performance: 'Comment m'avez-vous trouvé? [...] Bon? Moyen? Passable? Quelconque? Franchement mauvais?' His inability even to sustain his performance to the end — he undermines the lyric description of the sunset by a final 'C'est comme ça que ça se passe sur cette putain de terre' — knowing that it is meaningless, is a parallel to Hamm's consciousness of his incapacity as chessplayer. They both have a desperate need for

---

[3] Compare this with the following passage from *L'Innommable*, which throws an interesting light on the 'purpose' of suffering and its relation with story-telling. L'Innommable is speaking of 'ces Murphy, Molloy et autres Malone...': 'J'ai cru bien faire en m'adjoignant ces souffre-douleur. Je me suis trompé. Ils n'ont pas souffert mes douleurs, leurs douleurs ne sont rien, à côté des miennes, rien qu'une petite partie des miennes, celle dont je croyais pouvoir me détacher, pour la contempler' (7, p. 28).

play as a means of escape, but an inability to be taken in by
their own game.

They also however need an audience. Pozzo's theatricality
is to no purpose without witnesses — even though these
possess the destructive power of criticism, and can spoil the
performance by continuous interruption, as Pozzo finds with
Vladimir and Estragon (p. 69 of 1952 edition). They then
have to go through the game of begging him to continue, at
his insistence. The relationship between actor and audience is
even more essential in *Fin de partie*. 'A quoi est-ce que je
sers?' asks Clov. 'A me donner la réplique' answers Hamm.
He goes on to comment that he has made progress on his
story, but realising he does not have Clov's full attention,
forces him to join in a highly artificial dialogue in which Clov
asks Hamm how his story is getting on, and Hamm, playing
false modesty and hard-to-get, makes coy comments on its
progress. When he feels Clov is not involving himself sufficiently in the dialogue, he cries out angrily 'Mais pousse plus
loin, bon sang, pousse plus loin!' (p. 80).

There is a total breakdown in this way of any traditional
belief in the theatre as imitation of life. Our suspension of
disbelief is rudely interrupted at every turn. Just as Pirandello
had exposed the theatre for what it really is, emphasising the
divide between illusion and reality, and Brecht, with his
alienation-techniques, had underlined the very complex relationship between the theatre and real life, so Beckett is
constantly revealing his characters as actors, and his actors
playing a part in which they only half believe. By showing
the characters themselves to be conscious of playing a role,
and undermining that role at every turn, he creates a distance
between the various levels of actor, character and character-
playing-a-role which emphasises the illusion inherent in all
pure theatre. The 'sacred space' of play is used: but only to
be undermined. This in its turn serves as an image for one
of Beckett's central themes, the distance between the existent
and his own being. The story-telling, the time-filling are only
signs that existence is not its own end, but that the end,
whatever it might turn out to be, escapes all of Beckett's

characters without exception. Worm in *L'Innommable* perhaps gets the nearest to this ideal state — but Worm does not yet exist. And existence, though it is the fallen state *par excellence* for Beckett, is the only state that can be talked *about,* insofar as one can say anything meaningful about anything.

The difficulty of *saying* anything meaningful is perhaps one reason why Beckett turned to the drama as an alternative form. If you cannot say anything about existence, you can at least portray it, and nowhere better than in the theatre. As Robbe-Grillet pointed out in his essay on Beckett, 'Le personnage de théâtre *est en scène,* c'est sa première qualité: il est là' (*28,* p. 142). He may at the same time hold intelligent discourse with others on stage, he may perform a great number of varied actions, but all these are dependent on his actual stage presence, his 'being there'. In the 'slice of life' theatre, this fundamental presence is frequently masked: the aim is to create the illusion of reality as it is lived, and word, action — plot and physical gesture — are designed to obscure the fact of theatrical representation. But in a theatre such as Beckett's, such traditional props are stripped away, there is nothing to hide the fact that these characters are simply there. Robbe-Grillet says that in *Godot* 'tout se passe comme si les deux vagabonds se trouvaient en scène sans avoir de rôle' (*28,* p. 146). Perhaps it is rather that they *have* a role — we have seen the extent to which role-playing is important in both plays — but that this role is exposed for what it is at every moment. Traditional role-playing was designed to mimic known reality in one way or another: here it is simply a means of escape from an intolerable situation, but an escape which the characters know is doomed in advance. Hence the constant undermining by the characters themselves of the role they are playing, the cracks and faults constantly appearing in it, the disintegration into silence. The roles they adopt are not in any case sustained: tattered garments hastily donned to cover their nakedness, having already too obviously belonged to someone else.

The theme of 'being there' is reinforced in both plays by the constant reminder, made both implicitly and explicitly, that there is nowhere else to go. Didi and Gogo cannot escape,

either from each other or from their wait, because these are
the conditions of their existence. Godot is in this way not so
much the desired end of their waiting, but an image for
existence itself. Godot as an existent being is of dubious
reality, but their wait is the very fabric of their lives. Nothing
outside their stage presence has either reality or relevance; as
individuals they have neither past nor future, social being or
psychological substance. In *Fin de partie* the same idea of
everything being reduced to a single theatrical *now* operates
on two levels. 'Hors d'ici c'est la mort' says Hamm (p. 23),
and in a factual way we are led to believe this is true: Hamm
and Clov are the last survivors from some catastrophe, and
any remnants of life outside the refuge will soon disappear.
But at the same time they are creatures of the theatre: their
stage presence, where they wait, attempt to kill time, put off
the end, torture each other, is the only one they possess. So
when in reply to Hamm's question 'Pourquoi restes-tu avec
moi?' Clov says 'Il n'y a pas d'autre place' (p. 20), it can be
read on two levels, the factual and the metaphysical. The
apparent catastrophe which condemns them to the refuge is
a metaphor for the way in which they are condemned to
existence itself.

And yet at the same time as this stark 'being there', there
is a sense in which the characters are not there at all. Hamm
says 'Je n'ai jamais été là. [...] Absent, toujours' (pp. 97-8),
and Vladimir comments, after one of their 'little canters', 'On
trouve toujours quelque chose, hein, Didi, pour nous donner
l'impression d'exister?' (p. 97). Both are conscious of the
great void of unreality that opens out beneath their apparent
existence. They exist, in the sense that they go through all the
learned responses to their situation, they operate, somehow,
on a day-to-day level. But being eludes them, being which
would give them a sense of solidity and accomplishment. They
exist but they are not, since the self that they seek is always
and by definition beyond them. This tension, between the stark
existence which is what the audience witnesses, the sole
physical reality of an evening spent at the theatre, and the
sense of not-being that intrudes at every point in the plays, is

a major source of dramatic interest in Beckett's theatre, if one can speak in these terms of a feature so notably lacking in any conventional sense.

Whether the emphasis falls on existence or on non-being, the theatre, that place of illusion *par excellence,* is capable of giving it the most adequate expression. Not the theatre of rational discourse and consequent action, but the theatre of the simultaneous image, where the present is the only reality. On a stage where nothing happens, where the logic of cause and effect has been almost entirely broken down, what we are left with is a situation which does not depend for its understanding on progress in time or events in sequence. [4] This fact in its turn necessarily imposes very particular conditions upon the form of the drama.

---

[4] For an elaboration of this point, see *30,* p. 240.

3

Form, language

'Cette voix qui parle... qui ne s'écoute pas,
attentive au silence qu'elle rompt...'

(L'Innommable)

ORM, as we saw in Chapter 1, is of crucial importance to Beckett. What you say, as far as he is concerned, is governed entirely by how you say it, to the point where the how is the only legitimate preoccupation of the artist. The interpretation of the what, the domain of critics, is treated with impatience or frank disdain by Beckett.

A very revealing example of this preoccupation can be found in his comment on the passage from St Luke concerning the two thieves crucified with Christ, one of whom was saved, the other damned, which he uses in *Godot* (also in *Malone meurt*), and which in early criticism of the play was frequently given as an illustration of Beckett's Christian preoccupations. Beckett's own comment shows how it is a question of form above all that fascinated him:

> I take no sides. I am interested in the shape of ideas. There is a wonderful sentence in Augustine: 'Do not despair; one of the thieves was saved. Do not presume; one of the thieves was damned.' That sentence has a wonderful shape. It is the shape that matters. [1]

It is the linguistic formulation of the idea that catches Beckett's attention here, rather than the idea itself, the expression

---

[1] Quot. Alan Schneider, 'Waiting for Beckett', in *Beckett at 60: a festschrift,* Calder & Boyars, 1967, p. 34.

perhaps of the fundamental polarity of human existence rather than any explicitly Christian symbolism. (This polarity is taken up again later in the play when Godot's arrival is suddenly suspected; see Chapter 4). Such a polarity is a source of anguish to man: Vladimir's attempt to interest Estragon in the story is coupled with his query as to whether they should repent (p. 13), and clearly the mysterious and inexplicable nature of salvation and damnation is what interests him, but as an illustration of the polarity of life in general. Why should positive and negative, differenciation, exist at all? How can some things be classed as good and others bad? — by reference to what? Why should the lot of the two friends be suffering, when clearly happiness is at least a theoretical possibility? (This possibility is recognised by Hamm for example when he asks Clov: 'As-tu jamais eu un seul instant de bonheur?' — to which Clov of course replies in the negative — and in *Godot* Vladimir and Estragon hark back nostalgically to better times.)

The symmetry implicit in such a view of life is an important feature of *Godot* — indeed, it could be said to underlie its whole structure. The characters appear in pairs — as also of course in *Fin de partie* — each individual being totally dependent in one way or another on his partner, and much of the dialogue, which I will be looking at in more detail later in this chapter, depends on a symmetrical movement for its development. The play is composed of two equally balanced acts, echoing each other, but the changes that occur between the two — the tree sprouting leaves, Pozzo's blindness and Lucky's dumbness — are left mysterious and unexplained. Polarity solves nothing.

Symmetry is a feature also of *Fin de partie,* in its setting as well as in its imagery. The symmetry of the two high windows in the refuge to either side of the stage is underlined by Clov's first action, when he takes his stepladder and looks out of first one and then the other — giving an identical short laugh each time. Hamm's preoccupation with being in the centre presupposes a division of space into equal segments, as does of course the sustained chess-image throughout the play. The two camps oppose each other from either side of the board — 'Your war is the heart of the play', said Beckett to the actors playing Hamm and Clov in the London production (*18*, p. 468) — black opposing white, neither pole existing without the other.

The symmetry of the two acts of *Godot* is illustrative of another structuring device which has received considerable critical attention, that is its circularity. The end of Act II, being virtually identical to the end of Act I, is just sufficient to indicate an infinite succession into the future. Like the child who is satisfied and comforted by a single repetition of a story, Beckett's finely-tuned ear obviously realised that one act would be insufficient to convey endless repetition, three unnecessary. The endless wait, an image of life itself, which is the theme of the play, is thus exactly caught by its form. It is given emphasis by Vladimir's circular dog-song — the song whose beginning is in its end, and which therefore can be repeated *ad infinitum*. Beckett's interest in this song — originally German — can be traced back to a letter to Arland Ussher dated 11 July, 1937, and its formal implications are clearly exactly what Beckett needed to underline circularity in his play.

If the repetition of two acts is used to convey an endless process, repetition in general is a major structuring device in both plays. In *Godot* there are two main types of repetition: the repetition of certain actions, words, phrases, in the second act which have already been used in the first — Vladimir and Estragon's embrace when they meet in the morning, Estragon's nightmare, the Pozzo and Lucky episode, the discussion of whether to hang themselves — and, as a kind of ground bass, the constant reiteration of 'On attend ... Godot' or variations on that theme. While the former conveys endless recurrence of the same thing, the latter represents more than mere repetition: their wait is the very fabric of their existence, the one inescapable continuity in a world bereft of logical sequence and coherence. 'On attend Godot' is thus the repeated statement of an unchanging and unchangeable condition, the recall to reality from the endless diversions invented to escape from it.

Repetition in *Fin de partie* is if anything even more finely controlled and orchestrated. This is perhaps the most consciously ordered of all Beckett's plays, and was certainly worked on with more deliberate attention to overall form than *Godot* — which is perhaps why Beckett prefers it. 'There are no accidents in *Fin de partie*. Everything depends on analogy and repetition', he has said of it (*22*, p. 152), and the hard, implacable cruelty of much of its atmosphere is doubtless a result of this. Many of the repetitions underline the time theme: references to ending, elaborating on the title of the play, evocations of 'autrefois' or 'hier', or, indicating the mysterious process of continuity which can only be noted but not understood, 'Quelque chose suit son cours'. Sometimes the reference is to the gradual running-down process, giving rise to the repeated 'Il n'y a plus de ...' (nature, dragées, marée, navigateurs, calmant, plaids, cercueils etc.) — the comic effect of some of these being totally undermined by a kind of chill horror at what is actually going on. One of the most persistent repetitions is Clov's 'Je te quitte...', which acts as a refrain throughout the play — but which of course is never realised in action, except where it refers to his retreat to his kitchen. It is a kind of inversion of 'On attend Godot', in that it reveals the reverse of Clov's actual condition. One of the basic tensions of the play springs from his enslavement to Hamm's needs, and his desire to leave him, if only to his own little kitchen-world (from whose dimensions, 'trois mètres sur trois mètres sur trois mètres', he seems to derive a particular satisfaction). 'Clov has only one wish, to return to his kitchen', Beckett has stated. 'That must always be evident, as is Hamm's effort to detain him' (*22*, p. 153).

Beckett himself has thrown very interesting light on the whole question of repetition in his theatre, and the way in which he uses it as a fundamental structuring device in a play lacking the conventional 'props' of linear development of plot, character etc. In a comment on one of the productions with which he collaborated, he says

> Producers don't seem to have any sense of form in movement. The kind of form one finds in music, for

instance, where themes keep recurring. When, in a text, actions are repeated, they ought to be made unusual the first time, so that when they happen again —in exactly the same way — an audience will recognise them from before. In the revival of *Godot* [in Paris] I tried to get at something of that stylised movement that's in the play (*27*, p. 247).

The problems this might pose for actors reared in even a semi-naturalistic tradition are not hard to see. Beckett is clearly much more concerned about formal structure here than about creating an illusion of everyday reality. Roger Blin, in conversation with Tom Bishop, confesses to some of the difficulties he and his fellow-actors had with Beckett's requirements:

> Il avait sur sa pièce [*Fin de partie*] certaines vues qui empêchaient un peu de la jouer. Il voyait sa pièce comme une espèce de partition musicale, d'abord, quand un mot arrivait ou se répétait, quand Hamm appelait Clov, Clov devait revenir de la même manière chaque fois comme un truc musical par le même instrument et avec la même force (*19*, p. 145).

The reference to music, here and in the quotation from Beckett himself, is instructive, given the movement in all Beckett's work towards abstraction. Music is after all the most abstract, most formal and least referential of the arts. Stravinsky even claimed that music could never refer to anything outside itself, and that those who attempted to make it do so were falsifying its very nature. [2] Beckett seems to have a similar desire to do away with normal referential meaning, even though he is dealing in words which inevitably come charged with a whole referential context. The narrator of *L'Innommable,* as we have seen, wants to speak without meaning as a step along the road to the discovery of self, and

---

[2] See e.g. *Stravinsky in Conversation with Robert Craft,* Harmondsworth: Penguin Books, 1962, pp. 32-3.

Hamm seems to share his preoccupation in his desire to abolish meaning along with everything else. In Beckett's own involvement with the live theatre, one gets the impression that, in spite of the courtesy and consideration with which he reputedly treats them, actors are at best a necessary evil: he regards his own orchestration of his text as, if not fixed for all time, at least bearing its own inner logic and not to be played around with by self-indulgent performers wanting to be 'creative'. He told Deirdre Bair that his ideal play would be without actors (*18*, p. 513), and certainly the development of his theatre has given increasingly less scope for individual interpretation on the part of his actors. The score is set down in advance, and human reference of any kind is a positive hindrance to its proper execution. He is reputed at the present moment to be working on a new play for German television, with 'no name, and no dialogue, no words. [...] It's all movement, activity, percussion, cohesion'. [3]

This insistence on the importance of formal considerations (as opposed to what the text might appear to 'mean') for which he uses a musical analogy, goes a long way towards explaining Beckett's reluctance to encourage interpretations of his writing. The formal aspect of the words, both on the page and in performance, is paramount. In a letter to Schneider he made the following comment on *Fin de partie*:

> My work is a matter of fundamental sounds (no joke intended) made as fully as possible, and I accept responsibility for nothing else. If people want to have headaches among the overtones, let them. And provide their own aspirin. Hamm as stated, and Clov as stated, together as stated, nec tecum nec sine te, in such a place, and in such a world, that's all I can manage, more than I could (*16*, p. 185).

The sounds of language are particularly evident in for example the use of antiphonal dialogue in *Godot* (technically speaking 'stichomythia') — a device whose immediate origins

---

[3] Interview with Maeve Binchy, *Irish Times* (14.5.80), 7.

can again be traced to the music-hall (*27*, p. 245), and whose history is as old as theatre. But frequently Beckett manages to transform the glib patter of music-hall clowns into something with extraordinary evocative power, as in the following dialogue, worth quoting in full for the way in which Beckett manages to create a highly poetic effect with very ordinary means:

> Estragon — Toutes les voix mortes.
> Vladimir — Ça fait un bruit d'ailes.
> Estragon — De feuilles.
> Vladimir — De sable.
> Estragon — De feuilles.
>
> *Silence.*
> Vladimir — Elles parlent toutes en même temps.
> Estragon — Chacune à part soi.
>
> *Silence.*
> Vladimir — Plutôt elles chuchotent.
> Estragon — Elles murmurent.
> Vladimir — Elles bruissent.
> Estragon — Elles murmurent.
>
> *Silence.*
> Vladimir — Que disent-elles?
> Estragon — Elles parlent de leur vie.
> Vladimir — Il ne leur suffit pas d'avoir vécu.
> Estragon — Il faut qu'elles en parlent.
> Vladimir — Il ne leur suffit pas d'être mortes.
> Estragon — Ce n'est pas assez.
>
> *Silence.*
> Vladimir — Ça fait comme un bruit de plumes.
> Estragon — De feuilles.
> Vladimir — De cendres.
> Estragon — De feuilles.
>
> *Long silence.* (pp. 87-88)

Duckworth has noted the parallel with Dante here, claiming that Beckett's dead voices echo those of Dante's souls in Purgatory, and certainly the passage seems to hold more than is immediately obvious from its context (*2*, pp. lvii-lviii). In fact one of the mysterious attractions of this piece of dialogue is the way in which it goes beyond the rationally necessary, opening onto an unknown and uncharted world beyond the everyday. In the attempt to define the sounds from the 'other world', repetition plays a large part: Estragon by insisting on the suggestion he has just made closes the circle temporarily, and the dialogue lapses into silence before taking off on its spiralling course again, Vladimir's shift from 'd'avoir vécu' to 'd'être mortes' becomes a chord-change within the same melodic expression and harmonic progression.

The intricate interwoven pattern created by this kind of dialogue is quite different from that of much of the play, where the impression is given that neither is really listening to the other, and different again from the patterns of dialogue used in *Fin de partie*. There a significant part of Hamm and Clov's communication is based on contradiction and negation, as in the following passage (p. 55: other examples occur on pp. 20, 25 etc.) where the pattern is twice repeated, the 'contradiction' element being taken up first by one character then by the other, after an initial apparent opening to the other:

> Clov — Vous voulez donc tous que je vous quitte?
> Hamm — Bien sûr.
> Clov — Alors je vous quitterai.
> Hamm — Tu ne peux pas nous quitter.
> Clov — Alors je ne vous quitterai pas.
>
> *Un temps.*
>
> Hamm — Tu n'as qu'à nous achever. *(Un temps.)* Je te donne la combinaison du buffet si tu jures de m'achever.
> Clov — Je ne pourrais pas t'achever.
> Hamm — Alors tu ne m'achèveras pas.

Here the effect is not so much of a circular process closing into silence, as in the antiphonal dialogue of *Godot,* but of a vicious slamming of the door on the possibility of communication. It illustrates aptly the way in which all dialogue between Hamm and Clov is no more than an episode in their 'war'.

In both these examples, however, as significant as the dialogue itself is the silence which it breaks. On a purely formal level, Beckett's pauses, indicated in the stage directions by '*un temps*', are what rests are in a piece of music: they contribute to its shape and formal coherence. (Their orchestration is in fact much more precise than the printed text would suggest, since when Beckett is involved in production of his plays he times pauses to the exact second.) As in music, the totality of the work is composed of a juxtaposition of sound and silence, and as in music the one can have no significance or indeed existence without the other. The relationship between music and the theatre is of relevance here, since both, unlike 'literary' forms such as the novel, are 'performed arts', depending totally for their effect on the duration in time that they occupy. Michael Robinson has said that the theatre gave Beckett the opportunity 'to explore the blank spaces between the words' (*30*, p. 229), as opposed to the density of the printed page, and this is indeed the case, and an opportunity that Beckett has utilised to the full. On a metaphysical level Beckett's silences are at least as important as what he says: words are an illustration of the unsatisfactory nature of life itself, where reality is both unattained and unattainable. As Malone says, '...je me dis tant de choses, qu'y a-t-il de vrai dans tout ce babil? Je ne sais pas' (*8*, p. 115). In a situation where truth cannot be expressed, it is perhaps more truthful to remain silent — but silence is the one thing that Beckett's characters, whether in the novels or the plays, are unable to maintain, since silence is something that is earned by having spoken sufficiently, silence signifies the end that is longed-for yet never attained during life. Theodor Adorno has said of *Fin de partie* that it is a play tending towards silence, and his definition of its language could be applied equally well to *Godot*:

> The words have a makeshift sound because the silence was not wholly attained; they are the accompaniment to a stillness they disturb (*15*, p. 101).

But therein also lies the peculiar ambivalence of Beckett's attitude to language. Silence is certainly the ultimate goal pursued by all his characters, and yet, like Hamm both desiring death — and, it seems, the ultimate end of existence itself — and at the same time putting it off, spinning out his 'story' as long as possible, silence is feared, covered up, obliterated. After the antiphonal passage quoted above, Vladimir, unable to bear the silence any longer, cries out 'Dis quelque chose!' and, when Estragon fails to provide anything his anguish increases: 'Dis n'importe quoi!' (p. 88). Silence, the absence of sounds, is an image of the void, the backcloth against which all their actions are played out, but the void is incompatible with the time-element in which they have their existence, and as a result unbearable. I have already referred to the passage in Beckett's book on Proust, where he speaks of the moments when consciousness breaks through, moments when 'the boredom of living is replaced by the suffering of being' (*10*, p. 19). The 'boredom of living', the safety of the known, takes precedence however most of the time.

Anything is better than living consciously, as far as Beckett's characters are concerned. 'Dis n'importe quoi' becomes the impulse behind a great deal of the dialogue, in both *Godot* and *Fin de partie*. In *Godot* in particular, much of the language used is, on face value, extremely banal: it acquires depth only through the consciousness, ever-present, of what it is concealing. Although the passage of antiphonal dialogue quoted above has great evocative power, there are many instances of the same construction built entirely on cliché. For example:

> Vladimir — Question de tempérament.
> Estragon — De caractère.
> Vladimir — On n'y peut rien.
> Estragon — On a beau se démener.
> Vladimir — On reste ce qu'on est.
> Estragon — On a beau se tortiller.
> Vladimir — Le fond ne change pas.
> Estragon — Rien à faire.

(pp. 27-28)

The minor variations on the theme of incapacity in this passage
of dialogue have their impact not through the words themselves,
which are extremely banal, but through the image they create
of the universal human predicament. Faced with the funda-
mentals of birth and death, we *are* impotent, and our helplessness is underlined by our incapacity even to express it in other
than hackneyed phrases. All Beckett's characters are conscious
of using someone else's language which does not in fact convey
what they want it to. Maddie Rooney has the impression she
is using a 'dead language' [4] — hence perhaps the great stylisation
in the language of *All that fall,* an apparently naturalistic play
— and Clov is moved to violent reaction when Hamm mocks
his use of the word 'Hier' (p. 62).

> Hamm — Hier! Qu'est-ce que ça veut dire. Hier!
> Clov *(avec violence)* — Ça veut dire il y a un foutu bout
> de misère. J'emploie les mots que tu m'as appris. S'ils
> ne veulent plus rien dire apprends-m'en d'autres. Ou
> laisse-moi me taire.

Language is conceived here as having issued from Hamm. But
even when it is attributed to the anonymous 'they', as by the
narrator of *L'Innommable* ('rien que les paroles des autres',
p. 46), language is seen as essentially exterior to the individual,
part of the whole package imposed upon the self at birth, a
necessary evil in the messy business of existence.

This remoteness between the individual and the way in
which he expresses himself gives rise to another feature of
Beckett's drama, namely the divorce between what a given
character says and what he does. Again, the drama gave
Beckett an ideal opportunity to exploit the consciousness that
saying and doing were two quite separate occupations. As has
been pointed out frequently by critics (e.g. *21,* p. 29), Beckett
derived the formulation of this divorce from the occasionalist
philosopher Geulincx, whose development of the philosophy
of Descartes held that there was no necessary connection

4 *All that fall,* London: Faber & Faber, Pb. edn 1965, p. 35.

between phenomena of the mind, i.e. thoughts, and physical actions. The only interaction between them was miraculously caused by the intervention of God, who could act however only upon the body. The mind being completely autonomous, the rational course of action open to the individual was obviously to concentrate on this and leave mere bodily functions to divine purpose. For Geulincx, the system functioned perfectly because mind and body, like two exactly regulated clocks, were in fact in complete accord through the intervention of God. Beckett however retains only the fascination of the separation of the two, abandoning the hypothesis of an intervening God. Hence the frequent lack of relationship between what is said and what is done in Beckett's work.

A significant illustration of this, set down with characteristic comic seriousness, can be found in *Murphy* — to which Beckett apparently referred Colin Duckworth as a source when the latter was preparing his edition of *Godot* (2, p. xlvi). In it there is a passage where Murphy is described as 'split in two, a body and a mind. They had intercourse, apparently, otherwise he could not have known that they had anything in common. But he felt his mind to be bodytight and did not understand through what channel the intercourse was effected nor how the two experiences came to overlap. He was satisfied that neither followed from the other'. [5]

Murphy's curious situation is echoed many times in both *Godot* and *Fin de partie*. That Beckett himself recognised this, and wanted to emphasise it in stage performance, is shown by the fact that when he directed the Berlin production of *Fin de partie* he instructed that there should be a disjunction between gesture and dialogue: the actors were first to assume a physical attitude, then speak their lines (22, p. 154). The result must have been a highly stylised effect, and Beckett must have wanted to make the point very forcibly to require this of his actors. But it is in fact only an extension of a similar breakdown of relationship between language and action that is found in both plays. At the end of both acts of *Godot,* for instance,

---

[5] *Murphy,* London: Pan Books Ltd., 1973, p. 64.

they agree to leave, with Vladimir's final words 'Allons-y'. But in fact *Ils ne bougent pas.* A similar situation occurs in *Fin de partie,* where Clov's 'Je te quitte' is followed by inaction on his part (p. 106). A kind of extension of this can be seen in the way characters in both plays have trouble with their bodies: Vladimir has a bladder-problem, Estragon's feet are permanently sore, Hamm cannot stand up and Clov cannot sit down. When all four characters in *Godot* fall down during the episode with Pozzo and Lucky, they are unable to get up again, for no very apparent reason. One can only suppose that their bodies will no longer respond to the dictates of the mind. Like the clowns they resemble, their actions have become completely automatic, mechanical, but like machines they are imperfect and can break down.

One of the most startling illustrations of the automatism of the mind itself no longer connected to any kind of physical reality is Lucky's 'think'. As a speech it is given great prominence by being the only thing Lucky ever says, but it is such an extraordinary piece of writing that it would make considerable impact without that fact. The way in which it is delivered ('*débit monotone*') immediately takes it out of the region of normal speech, and yet it cannot be dismissed as a mere nonsense sequence. It in fact contains within it in parodied form many of the central themes of the play: the 'barbe blanche' of the 'Dieu personnel' recalls Godot's white beard as reported by the boy, and the inscrutable nature of salvation — the God '[qui] nous aime bien à quelques exceptions près on ne sait pourquoi' echoes Vladimir's preoccupation with the story of the thieves. The general decline of man — inexplicably, and in spite of all his technical progress — is again of course one of the underlying themes to the play. But whatever meaning one can attach to Lucky's stammerings, they have no *lived* meaning for Lucky or for anyone else, since they are patently not the expression in words of any kind of conviction on Lucky's part: they are turned on to order by his sadistic master, rapidly get out of control, and are only stopped when his hat is removed.

This grotesque parody of the function of language seems to be an extreme example only of what Beckett is trying to do all the time, as he turns his ear to 'fundamental sounds', refusing to project language more than is absolutely necessary into the reality it might represent. Even this 'absolutely necessary' is an element of failure for him, the ideal being, like that of l'Innommable, to speak and say nothing. And so his characters talk, fearful of the void that would be revealed by their silence, but what they say is essentially without significance, and although a form of dialogue is pursued, little communication is established. [6] This is illustrated in the opening lines of *Godot,* where Estragon's first words 'Rien à faire', referring to his problem with his boots, are taken up by Vladimir and given added meaning: 'Je commence à le croire', immediately establishing the theme of the futility of life in general. Here as elsewhere there is no real communication, their need one for the other is not consummated in a genuine verbal interchange, and if this is true of the characters of *Godot,* where something approaching normal friendship exists, how much more true it is of *Fin de partie,* built as it is on conflict, where the function of language is as weapon, to bludgeon the other party into surrender. [7]

The deliberate restrictions that Beckett puts around language as meaning, and his emphasis on the sounds of language, should warn us off any excessive symbol-hunting when it comes to the names of various characters. Critics have frequently been too hasty in assuming that all names *must* have a meaning — perhaps with a sidelong glance at Joyce, who

---

[6] An interesting early parallel to this breakdown in communication, where an apparent dialogue still persists, can be found in Voltaire's *Candide,* where he notes: 'Ils disputèrent quinze jours de suite, et au bout de quinze jours ils étaient aussi avancés que le premier. Mais enfin ils parlaient, ils se communiquaient des idées, ils se consolaient' (Ch. 20). Note too the role of consolation, which is a vital part of the relationship between Vladimir and Estragon.

[7] Contrast the function of language in Ionesco's *La Leçon,* where the word COUTEAU takes on physical properties and becomes the weapon itself.

made names bear such a heavy load of symbol and implication. [8] Beckett was perhaps asking for trouble when he called the centre of interest in his first play Godot, but why build interpretations around the Italian for 'well', *pozzo,* when Beckett is quite as likely to have been attracted by the round, rather harsh sound of the name? From his days as *lecteur* in Paris he would no doubt have retained the street name of the Ecole Normale Supérieure at St-Cloud — la rue Pozzo di Borgo. Hamm and Clov as hammer and nail is ingenious, but the addition of two further 'nails', Nagg and Nell, makes the whole thing too neat — while remaining annoyingly imprecise (see *23,* p. 233). Lucky may well be lucky — but this name could just as easily be a play on Lecky, a Dublin historian whose imposing statue Beckett would have passed every day in Trinity College.

'No symbols where none intended'; and whatever interpretations are offered, it is of paramount importance to retain the idea of the *sounds* of language when discussing what Beckett does with it. In the writing of his mature years, no word, however banal, is used accidentally or unconsciously, and as in music the overall formal effect is of the utmost concern. As R. Schechner has said, 'Beckett's genius in dialogue is his *scoring,* not his "book" ' (*27,* p. 274) — and this applies to the dialogue itself, to the relationship between dialogue and action, and to the ultimate rhythm of the plays in their entirety. As Molloy puts it, ironically,

> Ne pas vouloir dire, ne pas savoir ce qu'on veut dire, ne pas pouvoir ce qu'on croit qu'on veut dire, et toujours dire, voilà ce qu'il importe de ne pas perdre de vue dans la chaleur de la rédaction.

---

[8] We would do well to bear in mind Adorno's words, when he insists that 'Because nothing is simply that which is, everything seems to be the sign of something inward; yet the implicit inward referent no longer exists, and that is precisely the significance of the signs' (*15,* p. 91).

4

Time

'... ce monde sans visage sans
questions
où être ne dure qu'un instant
où chaque instant
verse dans le vide dans l'oubli
d'avoir été'

(Quatre poèmes)

THE impotence of language to say anything at all, coupled with the necessity to go on saying, reflects the basic dilemma of the artist for Beckett: imprisoned in time, in a flux which destroys as it carries along, the artist is nevertheless obliged to aim at the timeless and the permanent, conscious even as he creates of the inevitable failure of his enterprise. There is in this way a necessary stretching out towards some hypothetical future when the concept of the future itself will no longer apply. Language in the hands of the creative artist becomes a reflection of that process, or the process itself — 'le chemin vers l'avoir parlé', as Ludovic Janvier called *Fin de partie* (*26*, p. 174). There is a sense in which Beckett, like Proust, looked on life as 'l'exclusion hors de quelque essence éternelle' (*20*, p. 92), art being the means of recapturing that essence through escape from time. But as Ross Chambers points out, for Proust this escape was a real possibility, for Beckett it is not. Whereas Proust genuinely envisaged a kind of salvation through art, all that remains for Beckett is the compulsion to create, a compulsion mocked by its own hollow purposelessness. Hence the feeling of culpability that we have already had cause to note, culpability at life itself, hanging over so many of Beckett's characters, the sense of guilt at the one guiltless crime, the sin of being born. The exchange between

Vladimir and Estragon on repentance for this sin is echoed by the narrator of *L'Innommable* when he reflects on the possibility of having been given a pensum at birth, a punishment for having been born (p. 39), and taken up again in crueller form still by Clov, towards the end of *Fin de partie:* 'Je me dis — quelquefois, Clov, il faut que tu arrives à souffrir mieux que ça, si tu veux qu'on se lasse de te punir — un jour' (p. 108). [1] If the purpose of life, laid down by some mysterious 'other', is suffering, then clearly eventual escape is only possible through compliance with this purpose. For release it is necessary to conform and learn to 'suffer better' — a chilling example of Beckett's power over language through simple juxtaposition.

The consciousness which breaks through and provokes reflexions such as these is of course unbearable as a condition of existence. The 'boredom of living' is the common human experience, made up of countless rounds and rituals designed to keep awareness at bay. The use of such devices in *Godot* has been an object of frequent commentary, and it is probably unnecessary to rehearse each instance here — the games Vladimir and Estragon play with Lucky's hat, the relief at the 'divertissement' provided by Pozzo and Lucky, the way in which language itself becomes a mere instrument for making time pass: after one of their exchanges which has, like all the others, subsided into silence, Estragon comments 'Ce n'était pas si mal comme petit galop'. Vladimir replies 'Oui, mais maintenant il va falloir trouver autre chose' (p. 91). Their consciousness of their situation is crystallised in the following exchange: Vladimir — Nous sommes intarissables. Estragon — C'est pour ne pas penser (p. 87).

---

[1] A very similar idea is to be found in Schopenhauer: 'La vraie norme, pour juger un homme, c'est de dire qu'il est un être qui ne devrait pas exister mais qui expie son existence par d'innombrables souffrances et par la mort. Que peut-on attendre d'un tel être? Ne sommes-nous pas tous des pécheurs condamnés à mort? Ce que nous expions, d'abord par la vie et ensuite par la mort, c'est le fait d'être né' (*La Naissance de la philosophie à l'époque de la tragédie grecque,* trans. Geneviève Bianquis, Paris: Gallimard, Coll. Idées, p. 40).

But the point should perhaps be made that what Beckett is underlining here is the subjective nature of time: time is not a fixed continuum into which we slot in a predictable way, but a fluid, shifting medium which is more often than not incomprehensible. The 'divertissement' is one of the few ways in which man can actually manipulate time, make its experience shorter or longer according to the way it is filled. After Pozzo and Lucky have departed, Vladimir comments 'Ça a fait passer le temps', to which Estragon replies 'Il serait passé sans ça'. Vladimir rejoins 'Oui. Mais moins vite' (p. 66). And on the second appearance of Pozzo and Lucky, Vladimir comments joyfully: 'Déjà le temps coule tout autrement' (p. 109).

The way in which time can be manipulated is obvious too in the story-telling urge of many of Beckett's characters, which is illustrative too of a profound ambiguity in their approach to time and to the hypothetical end of time. As we saw in Chapter 2, the telling of stories such as Hamm's is not a purely autobiographical exercise related to the past, but projects much more profoundly and more urgently into the future. It is a reflection of the search for the self, the attempt to grasp that unattainable essence that would make sense of experience. You must go on saying words 'tant qu'il y en a, il faut les dire, jusqu'à ce qu'ils me trouvent, jusqu'à ce qu'ils me disent' (7, p. 213). Story-telling is thus a way of advancing the end, both by doing the thing that is necessary to bring it about, and by providing a distraction which makes time seem to pass more quickly. Hamm for example confides his worry to Clov that his story will soon be finished, that there will be no other way of 'filling in' time, to which Clov retorts 'Bah tu en feras une autre' (p. 83). (The same anxiety in more acute form is present in Winnie in *Oh les beaux jours,* who carefully apportions actions and objects to various points in the day, so that she does not run out of means to hide the void of her life before the end of each day.) But it is also a way of putting off the end: the control, albeit illusory, that Hamm thinks he has over this aspect of time is indicated in his 'Il est temps que cela finisse et cependant j'hésite encore à [...] finir' (p. 17).

If the theme of story-telling in its double relationship to time underlies a great deal of Beckett's writing, the search for the self is given particularly clear symbolic form in *Fin de partie* in Beckett's use of the heap-idea. There are two references to it in the play, firstly Clov's opening words: 'Fini, c'est fini, ça va finir, ça va peut-être finir. *(Un temps.)* Les grains s'ajoutent aux grains, un à un, et un jour, soudain, c'est un tas, un petit tas, l'impossible tas' (pp. 15-16). Hamm takes up the reference later (p. 93), when he reflects 'Instants sur instants, plouff, plouff, comme les grains de mil de ... ce vieux Grec, et toute la vie on attend que ça vous fasse une vie'. Beckett himself claims to have forgotten who exactly he meant by 'ce vieux Grec', but it seems likely, in terms of the train of thought involved, to be an amalgam of the pre-Socratic Zeno with one of his lesser-known followers, Eubulides of Miletus. Eubulides continued Zeno's meditation on the incompatibility of unity and plurality, the finite and the infinite, and one of his demonstrations was that known as 'the Heap'. The question is: at what point does a number of grains of wheat become a heap? (It seems that Eubulides used wheat-grains rather than millet as his illustration.) If two grains do not constitute a heap, what about four? Or ten? Or one hundred? What is the crucial point at which the quantitative process of adding grain to grain effects a qualitative change in the result, i.e. when does the addition of single units become a heap? This is clearly a problem which preoccupies Beckett in this play: we wait eternally for the 'instants sur instants' to add up to something that is recognisably 'une vie'. All we can know are the passing moments, and there is no reason, logically, why these moments should ever become something qualitatively different, 'a life'. The self, representing the wholeness which our fragmented everyday perception belies, is necessarily beyond our reach: the one and the many are of different orders, and irreconcilable. Once again, the idea receives more extended and less symbolic treatment in *L'Innommable,* where the narrator reflects that 'les secondes passent, les unes après les autres, saccadées, ça ne coule pas, elles ne passent pas, elles arrivent, pan, paf, pan, paf [...] il y en a qui les ajoutent

les unes aux autres pour en faire une vie, moi je ne peux pas...'
(p. 181).

Since the end to life is unattainable, all we can know are
the passing moments, the waiting that takes on meaning only
through the addition of the impossible 'for', the situation in
which, as Walter A. Strauss puts it, 'l'attente de Godot n'est
plus que le "correlatif objectif" de la condition humaine' (*19*,
p. 278). The idea of waiting, coupled with that of guilt for an
unknown crime which we have already looked at, explains
Beckett's fascination for the figure of Dante's Belacqua, condemned to live out his life again in the ante-purgatory through
having left repentance too late. Belacqua is for Beckett the
archetype of enforced idleness, but whereas Belacqua is truly
sorry for his tardiness, and believes in the goal of purgatory
he has been set, Beckett keeps only the form and the nostalgia
for a purpose he has no faith in.

Time viewed in the perspective of the ante-purgatory is
essentially duration, a kind of featureless eternal present lacking
distinguishing characteristics. In terms of dramatic technique
this is immediately conveyed in both *Godot* and *Fin de partie*
by the total lack of recognisable plot. 'Rien ne se passe,
personne ne vient, personne ne s'en va, c'est terrible', says
Estragon (pp. 57-58). Both he and Vladimir have lost their
sense of the individuality of each passing day: they cannot for
example remember what day it is (p. 18), and even the day's
interlude between Acts I and II belongs to mythical rather
than 'real' time. In *Fin de partie,* Clov's only response to
Hamm's query 'Quelle heure est-il?' is 'La même que d'habitude' (p. 18). Duration is seen as a formless and mysterious
process in which even the individual is described in abstract
terms. Clov's usual 'Quelque chose suit son cours' becomes on
one occasion 'Je suis mon cours' (p. 60), announced this time
by Hamm. The impersonal formlessness of being in time is
also conveyed by Clov's oblique 'Ça avance' — an indication
that progress of a kind is being made, though so ill-defined
and apparently remote from their existence that no impression
is conveyed of actual movement in time. Each day is like its
predecessors: 'C'est une fin de journée comme les autres'

(p. 28). Hamm makes an attempt to break the day up into sections by the various episodes of his story, or by his repeated 'Ce n'est pas l'heure de mon calmant?' — but it is significant that he only wants forgetfulness of his present intolerable situation. The uniformity of their experience of time and situation is again explicit in Estragon's anti-Platonic outburst, when Vladimir asks him if he doesn't recognise the spot where they have again met to wait for Godot. 'Reconnais! Qu'est-ce qu'il y a à reconnaître? J'ai tiré ma roulure de vie au milieu des sables! Et tu veux que j'y voie des nuances! *(Regard circulaire.)* Regarde-moi cette saloperie! Je n'en ai jamais bougé!' (pp. 85-86).

There are indeed changes indicated in both plays. In *Fin de partie,* change is described essentially in terms of decline or loss. 'Mais nous respirons, nous changeons! Nous perdons nos cheveux, nos dents! Notre fraîcheur! Nos idéaux!' says Hamm (p. 25). Supplies are gradually running out — no more pain-killer, bicycles, nature etc. In *Godot* the theme of decay is present especially in Lucky's speech — 'l'homme [...] malgré le progrès [...] est en train de maigrir [...] de rapetisser [...] rétrécir' (pp. 60-61), but also in the sudden blindness of Pozzo and Lucky's dumbness. This latter reveals another characteristic of change in the play: it is inexplicable. Pozzo himself can explain neither the why nor the when, much to Vladimir's disappointment, and is infuriated by Vladimir's demands for precision: 'Vous n'avez pas fini de m'empoisonner avec vos histoires de temps? C'est insensé! Quand! Quand! Un jour, ça ne vous suffit pas, un jour pareil aux autres, il est devenu muet, un jour je suis devenu aveugle, un jour nous deviendrons sourds, un jour nous sommes nés, un jour nous mourrons, le même jour, le même instant, ça ne vous suffit pas?' (p. 126).

The same incomprehensibility with regard to change is present in the sudden transformation of the tree between the first and second acts. Beckett himself has said that he directed that the tree should put on leaves merely to indicate the passage of time. But if this is simply meant as a stylistic device, it fails to carry Vladimir with it, as he is highly puzzled by the change in the tree. It is another arbitrary feature in an arbitrary world, and the precariousness of their grasp of the time interlude is indicated by Estragon's forgetting that it was 'yesterday' when they were last in the same spot.

The fundamental images of both plays thus tend towards an abolition of time as ordered and comprehensible change towards a rationally definable object. As I noted earlier (Chapter 2), Beckett's is a theatre of situation, to be grasped as one would an abstract painting, without reference to any sequential movement. And yet theatre and music are of all the arts the most subject to time — the spoken word, the language of gesture and so forth depend on time for their very articulation. An evening in the theatre is a symbol of our submission to time. Hence a very positive tension in Beckett's plays which echoes that running through his work as a whole, an inevitable failure underlying apparent triumph, time regained being only the appearance set against the reality of time lost.

Time in the sense of duration is however our element, and Beckett's characters frequently display an inclination to keep things as they are. I have noted above (p. 54) Hamm's hesitation on his 'ending': he both desires the end and wants to put it off for as long as possible. As Beckett said of him, he is the bad chess-player who knows the game is lost, but wants to carry on making senseless moves to put off the final moment of defeat. Vladimir and Estragon echo this fundamental ambivalence in their reactions when they think that a noise nearby may be the arrival of Godot: Vladimir's immediate reaction is one of joy — 'Nous sommes sauvés!', whereas Estragon is struck with panic: 'Je suis damné!' (p. 104). Beckett has clearly identified a very basic human dilemma here: we are all waiting, and as such projecting into the future, with plans, hopes, dreams. And yet as we do this we are wishing our lives away. Camus has caught admirably the same ambivalence in *Le Mythe de Sisyphe,* where he equates it with the feeling of the absurd:

> Un jour vient [...] et l'homme constate ou dit qu'il a trente ans. Il affirme ainsi sa jeunesse. Mais du même coup, il se situe par rapport au temps. Il y prend sa place. Il reconnaît qu'il est à un certain moment d'une

courbe qu'il confesse devoir parcourir. Il appartient au temps et, à cette horreur qui le saisit, il y reconnaît son pire ennemi. Demain, il souhaitait demain, quand tout lui-même aurait dû s'y refuser. [2]

Although Beckett in his rare comments on his work has tended to stress the negative pole of this dilemma — Hamm wilfully putting off the end, for example — the positive pole is at least as strong, especially in *Fin de partie*. It is in fact responsible for some of the touches of sick humour that survive in this bleak world. The flea that Clov finds in his trousers is pursued relentlessly, since 'à partir de là l'humanité pourrait se reconstituer' (p. 50). The idea is continued in the episode where Clov, having found and half-killed a rat in the kitchen, when he was interrupted by Hamm, says he must go back to the kitchen, since 'si je ne tue pas ce rat il va mourir' (p. 90). Hamm's first reaction to the mysterious boy sighted outside the window, looking (at least in the French version) like a Buddha figure or the dying Moses, is to kill him as potential procreator; he decides against it only with the thought that if the boy remains outside he will die anyway. Every vestige of life must be stamped out, since only in this way can the end, the void, Clov's dream be realised of a world 'où tout serait silencieux et immobile et chaque chose à sa place dernière, sous la dernière poussière' (p. 78). Meaning itself must be extinguished — for it is surely a sudden fear that motivates Hamm's question 'On n'est pas en train de ... signifier quelque chose?' (p. 49), a suggestion which Clov immediately ridicules: 'Signifier? Nous, signifier! *(Rire bref.)* Ah elle est bonne!' Hamm is like l'Innommable in his desire to speak and say nothing (7, p. 27), and in his realisation of the difficulty of this enterprise — a little meaning always manages to creep in.

The ambivalence in Beckett's attitude to the notion of ending reflects a further one, that between time as endlessly long and time that is over before you have been able to seize

---

2 Camus, *Le Mythe de Sisyphe* in *Essais,* Paris: Gallimard, Bibl. de la Pléiade, 1965, p. 107.

what it is bearing along. The endlessness of time is perhaps
the more apparent in both plays, since it is their very fabric.
In both cases dramatic tension is created, not by our wondering
whether or not the end will be realised — whether Godot will
come, whether Hamm will die or Clov leave him — but from
our perception of this endless wait for an object which is by
definition unattainable. But against the dilation of time implicit
in this backcloth, some of Beckett's most startlingly beautiful
images concern the fleeting character of life. Immediately after
Pozzo's outburst on time quoted above, for example, he goes
on: 'Elles accouchent à cheval sur un tombeau, le jour brille un
instant, puis c'est la nuit à nouveau' (p. 126). Vladimir takes
up the image on Pozzo's departure: 'A cheval sur une tombe
et une naissance difficile. Du fond du trou, rêveusement, le
fossoyeur applique ses fers' (p. 128). Midwife and grave-
digger are one and the same, since birth contains death within
it. However, as he goes on, 'On a le temps de vieillir. L'air est
plein de nos cris.' In our brief existence we have time only to
age and to suffer, being caught up in the process of dying
from the moment of birth. 'La fin est dans le commencement
et cependant on continue' (*4*, p. 91). The same sort of contrast
between the endlessness of time and — here at least — the
desirable brevity of life is evoked in a little-known poem of
Beckett's where he writes of the moment when

> je n'aurai plus à fouler ces longs seuils mouvants
> et vivrai le temps d'une porte
> qui ouvre et se referme   (*19*, p. 45)

The instantaneous nature of life viewed in a certain perspective explains in part the unreliable character of memory
as illustrated by many of Beckett's characters. Past events flow
away before one has had a chance to grasp them, identify them,
relate them one to another. 'On ne descend pas deux fois dans
le même pus', says Estragon (p. 84), parodying Heraclitus
and the notion of ever-changing flux. So the boy who comes
at the end of each act does not recognise Vladimir, although
the latter is at first sure it is the same one who brought the

message from Godot the previous evening (pp. 70, 129). On
the second day Estragon does not remember the tree, and only
has vague memories of Pozzo and Lucky. The void into which
yesterday has already sunk is a source of anguish to Vladimir
who tries, in vain, to get Estragon to remember what they did
(pp. 91-94). Pozzo by his second appearance has forgotten
having seen the two friends the previous day, justifying himself
by claiming that 'les aveugles n'ont pas la notion du temps'
(p. 122).

Even where past events are remembered, the categories of
time are destroyed, so that events remain essentially unrelated
and lack any kind of temporal depth and solidity. When Hamm
mocks Clov for his use of the word 'hier' — 'Qu'est-ce que ça
veut dire? Hier!', Clov replies with a bitter definition: 'Ça veut
dire il y a un foutu bout de misère' (p. 62). Time is only
definable in terms of the suffering it occasions. Where there are
apparent memories of past events, these are impossible to in-
terpret, since the present, conscious self is no longer the one
who experienced them. 'Demain', asks Vladimir, 'quand je
croirai me réveiller, que dirai-je de cette journée? Qu'avec
Estragon mon ami, à cet endroit, jusqu'à la tombée de la nuit,
j'ai attendu Godot? Que Pozzo est passé, avec son porteur, et
qu'il nous a parlé? Sans doute. Mais dans tout cela qu'y
aura-t-il de vrai?' (p. 128). The past will not lie still under our
analytic gaze, its formless chaos is not susceptible to our urge
to codify, classify, and understand.

Small wonder then that this sort of consciousness is kept
for anguishingly privileged moments. The rest of the time we
submit and do not ask too many questions. Faced by total
flux, Pozzo tries to hang on to his sanity by keeping his sense
of clock-time: his watch is clearly one of his most important
possessions, and its physical massiveness, its *presence,* is a sign
of its status in Pozzo's hierarchy of values. But in Act II he
loses it, part of the general deterioration towards timelessness
that characterises the movement of the play.

Universal flux is thus one perspective on time in these
plays. But in another, equally real sense, time does not seem
to *pass* at all. The heap image in *Fin de partie* is illustrative

of this: the seconds pile up, and we wait in vain for the thing called 'a life' to emerge. But it is characteristic that the accumulation of time is not for Beckett a happy or enriching experience. We have only to think of the heap under which Winnie is buried in *Oh les beaux jours* to feel its claustraphobic, engulfing presence, or consider the extended version of the image in *L'Innommable* (p. 171):

> ... on peut se le demander [...] pourquoi le temps ne passe pas, ne vous laisse pas, pourquoi il vient s'entasser autour de vous, instant par instant, de tous les côtés, de plus en plus haut, de plus en plus épais, votre temps à vous, celui des autres, celui des vieux morts et des morts à naître, pourquoi il vient vous enterrer à compte-gouttes ni mort ni vivant, sans mémoire de rien, sans espoir de rien, sans connaissance de rien, sans histoire ni avenir, enseveli sous les secondes, racontant n'importe quoi, la bouche pleine de sable...

Beckett is about as far here as he could be from any idea of looking back over a life and making sense of it. Precisely because the 'heap' is an impossible one, all that is perceptible are the undifferentiated grains which refuse meaning in terms both of the past and the future.

Yesterday may be incomprehensible, but it is unavoidably there: as Beckett says in the essay on Proust, 'Yesterday is not a milestone that has been passed, but a daystone on the beaten track of the years, and irremediably part of us, within us, heavy and dangerous' (*10,* p. 13). We *are* the sum of our experiences, but this sum remains inexplicable, a mere burden rather than an enlightenment. There is a sense also in which Beckett wants us to see this present past as a kind of dead, haunting presence within us, rather than something that grows with us. This surely is the meaning of Vladimir's disjointed reflection on thought (pp. 89-90):

> Vladimir — Ce n'est pas le pire, de penser.
> [...]
> Vladimir — Ce qui est terrible, c'est d'avoir pensé.
> Estragon — Mais cela nous est-il jamais arrivé?

> Vladimir — D'où viennent tous ces cadavres?
> Estragon — Ces ossements.
> [...]
> Vladimir — On a dû penser un peu.
> Estragon — Tout à fait au commencement.
> Vladimir — Un charnier, un charnier.

Thought itself is seen as a kind of graveyard, littered with useless, dried-up bones bereft of all living flesh. Bleached skeletons of the mind, past thoughts will neither go away nor assist in the present process of thought. More menacing than merely useless, they haunt the charnel-house of rationality as a constant reminder of its demise.

Once again therefore Beckett presents opposites — in this case flux and the piling-up of the past — as the twin poles of a single reality. It is vitally important in any approach to Beckett's work to realise that he is frequently presenting what appear to be contradictory view-points — not from any desire for rational argument on the subject, but because his poetic vision embraces first and foremost the contradictions of existence. We *are* both impatient with time that appears to move too slowly, and fearful of the end. The past is both outside our grasp and a menacing presence within us. What Beckett gives us is a sense of mythical time that is outside normal temporal categories, but not in the way in which classical theatre escaped these categories. In the classical theatre the conventions are based on concentration. The time of the action (up to several years) is concentrated into plot-time (twenty-four hours), which is itself concentrated into the time of the actual performance (two hours). Beckett, freed from historical, clock-time, gives us an essential timelessness, but a timelessness bearing a weight of temporality that few writers have equalled.

5

Tragi-comedy

> 'le rire des rires [...] le rire qui rit du rire [...]
> qui salue la plaisanterie suprême, en un mot —
> le rire qui rit [...] de ce qui est malheureux'
>
> *(Watt)*

THE ambivalence present in Beckett's handling of the theme
of time — the sense of the eternal present instant jux-
taposed with endless duration — finds formal expression in a
certain ambivalence in the very *genre* Beckett chose to present
this vision. *Godot* is called in the English version 'A tragicomedy in two acts', stating immediately the particular mixture
which informs the play, and although *Fin de partie* does not
bear any sub-title the same definition could be applied to it,
if the increased grey starkness of its tone is taken into consideration. But whereas the opposing poles of the time-theme
are necessarily presented separately — thus betokening their
very submission to time in its form of duration — Beckett has
managed to produce an almost total fusion between the tragic
and the comic elements. It is in this that these plays differ
from the classical *genre* of tragicomedy, which grew up in
seventeenth-century Spain as a reaction against the Greco-
Roman tradition of total separation between the *genres,* and
which consisted of an alternation within a single play of tragic
and comic situations. [1] If one wants to find an exception to
this rule of alternation, one must turn to Shakespeare, whose
all-embracing genius perceived the underlying relationship
between the tragic and the comic. So we have for example a

---

[1] On this point see Alfonso Sastre, 'Seven Notes on *Waiting for
Godot*, *11*, p. 103.

powerful interplay of both elements in *King Lear,* especially perhaps in the scene on the heath, where Lear's rageful despair is both undercut and given added significance by the Fool's comically wise patter.

In the same way, what Beckett wants to say is neither purely tragic in the classical sense — I shall return to this point — nor purely comic, and his fusion of the two has resulted in a third, totally different mood which one may qualify as the 'grotesque' (see *36,* pp. 104 ff.). Where classical tragedy derived its force from a conflict with the absolute, the grotesque, in a world deprived of absolutes, is a manifestation of absurdity. Tragedy imposes a choice upon man between two conflicting orders, the human and the divine: as Jan Kott says, 'the tragic situation becomes grotesque when both alternatives of the choice imposed are absurd, irrelevant or compromising. The hero has to play, even if there is no game' (*36,* p. 107). In such a situation, comic elements are always a manifestation of something darker, more sinister and more desperate, while the tragic is constantly undercut by the knowledge that protest, indeed suffering itself, is futile.

One of the most obvious manifestations of this ambivalence is the suggestion of clowning, especially in *Godot.* Much of the humour of *Godot* derives from the mechanical quality of speech and gesture. Like that of clowns, the behaviour of the characters in this play is funny because it somehow does not belong to them, there is a distance between their real selves and the actions they perform. We have already seen (Chapter 3) the extent to which their language is 'borrowed', and this applies equally well to their actions. Incapable of 'being' their true selves, their movements display their alienation through physical incapacity, inability to perform simple actions, unwarranted clumsiness. The grotesque incapacity of Nagg and Nell in their dustbins to accomplish even the simplest of everyday actions is only an extreme statement of what all Beckett's characters suffer from. There is frequently a total lack of spontaneity: Pozzo for example seems capable of action only if he is begged to do something, as when he gets Vladimir and Estragon to urge him to sit down, being unable to accomplish this very ordinary act otherwise (p. 50). Lucky's speech derives its humour from the total divorce between his physical being and what he is — in vain — trying to convey, but it is a humour that can only be described as grotesque. It is interesting that in his role as 'knouk' he seems to parody the traditional role of the fool. But whereas the fool had a wisdom far beyond that of his master, Pozzo can only refer back desperately to the days when Lucky taught him all he knew.

The physical manifestations of the grotesque, for which the theatre is so admirably suited, are everywhere present in the play. Lucky's dance is only one instance of a constant exploitation of the theatre's resources in this direction. The use of slapstick, pratfalls, all the traditional business of the clown, are here given an enlarged dimension by being infused with a sense of the reality of what is happening on stage. The refractory nature of things, Estragon's boots, Vladimir's inability to laugh without causing himself pain, the usual paraphernalia of the humourist are here used to reinforce a sense of metaphysical exile. In the same way, when Lucky kicks out at Estragon who is trying to console him (p. 44), what we have is more than pure slapstick, a commentary on the incommunicability of pity, the necessary suffering in any contact between human beings — but the whole thing is undercut by Estragon's childish gesture immediately preceding, and by his comic hopping around in pain afterwards. The episode is given added point when Beckett presents its mirror-image in Act II: Estragon's hopping this time is caused by him hurting his foot when he kicks Lucky in revenge (p. 124). We, the audience, are allowed no indulgence in our sympathy for either Lucky or Estragon, being immediately lifted onto a higher plane to perceive the universality of suffering, and its total futility. It is derisory, rather than ennobling.

Suffering always seems somehow inadequate and ignoble: we must learn to suffer *better*. The tragic is never allowed the kind of expression which would give it purpose and nobility. For instance, Estragon's movingly simple statement 'Je suis malheureux' when he is unable to make sense of the arrival of the boy (p. 70), is bitterly countered by Vladimir's riposte: 'Sans blague! Depuis quand?'

This rigorous anti-sentimentality, the refusal of any kind of indulgence, is present also in the abrupt changes of mood which occur throughout, resulting in incongruous juxtapositions and bathos. Vladimir and Estragon's embrace is cut short by physical disgust: 'Tu pues l'ail!' says Estragon (p. 21). Pozzo's elevated speech on the sunset disintegrates into disgust at the general situation (p. 52). And these changes in mood are only a kind of staggered representation of the universal parody which is at the heart of both plays. The characters, being unable to *be* in any authentic sense, can only parody the actions and the emotions of others. Both Hamm and Pozzo are pure parody, especially where the emotions are concerned. Hamm's demand that Clov should say something 'from the heart' before he leaves is a grotesque comment on their relationship, founded as it is on warring hatred. In the same way, Pozzo's comment to Vladimir, 'Nous finirons par nous prendre en affection' (p. 39), only makes more evident his total inability to feel affection for any other being. More poignant perhaps is the 'Je suis content' routine (p. 84) where the two friends' expression of satisfaction at being together again both fails to convey and goes beyond their actual feelings.

The use of verbal humour and the telling of jokes is a specifically verbal form of Beckett's tragicomic vision. The verbal play on 'ouïe/oui' (suggested by Nell's 'non') is given depth in the conflict between what is being said and Nagg and Nell's situation, which in its turn serves to underline their general decrepitude (pp. 30-1). The story about the tailor told by Nagg is a brilliant example of an apparently comic tale given tragic dimension through the direct comment it makes on the general condition of the universe: the tailor's short-comings are as nothing compared with the incompetence of the Creator. But here as elsewhere the general comment and its profound significance are undercut by their comic context, and Beckett does not allow himself a direct statement of the tragic.

This kind of indirect statement on the inadequacy of our reactions in the face of suffering is present also in Pozzo's comment when Vladimir and Estragon are hesitating over wiping away Lucky's tears: 'Dépêchez-vous. Bientôt il ne pleurera plus' (p. 44). There is here the same sort of sadistic desire to be 'in on' suffering as we find in Clov's comment on the half-dead rat: 'Si je ne tue pas ce rat il va mourir' (p. 90). The terrible humour of such a statement does not allow for any sentimentality, regarding either death itself or more particularly human response to it, which must necessarily fall far short of the enormity of the phenomenon itself. In the normal humorous situation, the self becomes spectator, and laughter is provoked by this distanciation between the self and what it sees. Beckett's characters accomplish this exteriorisation, stand back and see themselves as actors — but then are struck with horror at what they see. They are then however thrown back by this very perception to the derisory nature of their situation, which can be neither genuinely tragic nor genuinely comic.

Such humour, if indeed it can be called humour, is necessarily destructive. All humour is negative in this sense, critical rather than constructive, but Beckett's humour goes beyond the merely critical to the point where it destroys everything it touches. The comic and the tragic come together in a vicious clasp in the passage from *Watt* quoted at the beginning of this chapter, where Beckett gives his definition of the *'risus purus'* — 'le rire qui rit [...] de ce qui est malheureux'. [2] Gone are our polite defences against the suffering of an innocent world, gone our intellectual responses which allow us to rationalise — or to laugh at something else, the fundamental response to the whole gigantic farce of living can only be, must be, derision. Beckett picks up the same theme in *Fin de partie* and gives it dramatic force in the following dialogue between Nagg and Nell. Nell is shocked at Nagg's mockery of Hamm's predicament:

Nell — Rien n'est plus drôle que le malheur, je te l'accorde. Mais —

[2] *Watt,* Paris: Edns de Minuit, 1968, p. 49.

Nagg *(scandalisé)* — Oh!
Nell — Si, si, c'est la chose la plus comique au monde.
   Et nous en rions, nous en rions, de bon cœur, les
   premiers temps. Mais c'est toujours la même chose.
   Oui, c'est comme la bonne histoire qu'on nous ra-
   conte trop souvent, nous la trouvons toujours bonne,
   mais nous n'en rions plus (pp. 33-4).

Once again the potentially tragic status of suffering is undercut;
suffering is funny, but it is also boring after a time. It partakes
of the universal monotony of life in general, and like an excess
of television horror documentary, it numbs us after a while, so
that although we know we should be reacting, we are unable
to produce more than a parody of genuine emotion.

If there is a tragic element in these plays therefore, it is a
kind of shadow-image of what has usually been understood
as tragedy. Classical tragedy, whether in its Greek form or its
subsequent evolution through the European theatre, has gen-
erally involved some kind of a breakdown of order: man falls
because he has somehow, usually unknowingly or against his
will, violated the order laid down by divine will. Phèdre for
example is moved against her will — though as in all true
tragedy the force that compels her is in fact within her — to
violate the inviolable nature of things. But in Beckett this is
not the case, since there is no order to violate. The universe
is abandoned to the principle of the arbitrary, one can never
know whether one has broken the rules or not, since no law
is ever communicated unambiguously. [3] One thief was saved,
the other was damned — and their roles could have been
reversed. This kind of consciousness is in fact beyond pessimism, as instanced by Schopenhauer for example, since
pessimism requires a world-order, a necessary framework
within which things are bound to exist. The terrifying feature
of Beckett's universe is that there is *no* discernable order, no
way in which man can assess what he should and should not
do, no destiny except certain death. 'Il n'y a plus de nature'

---

[3] On the whole question of order and the arbitrary, and its
relationship with the tragic consciousness, see *37, passim.*

says Clov (p. 25), 'nature' being the instance *par excellence* of order, of a predictable, seasonal cycle of events. Human nature itself disappears in uncertainty, when individuals cannot be recognised from one day to the next.

Such a consciousness can have only a negative expression: in these two plays it tends to be definable through negative experience, suffering, cruelty, and so forth, or simple negation. Suffering is the universal against which the whole movement of the plays takes place. In what is reputedly Beckett's favourite line of *Fin de partie* he transforms Descartes's affirmation of the primacy of the intellect into an existential statement of the primacy of suffering: 'Il pleure' says Clov of Nagg. 'Donc il vit' replies Hamm (p. 84). Suffering itself is not tragic: it is rather the incomprehensible pointlessness of it that gives it special status, as does man's total inadequacy in the face of it. 'Tous ces blessés à mort, avec quelle science on les soigne', says Clov (p. 108), recalling perhaps Beckett's own wartime experience in a Red Cross hospital in France. What point is there in human knowledge, when it serves only to prolong an agony that will end in certain death?

One reaction to the total helplessness of such a situation is to create an illusion of power through a sadistic imposition on the less powerful. Pozzo's relationship with Lucky is a clear example of this, as is that between Hamm and Clov. If the world in general is uncontrollable, at least one can wield power in a limited way with another human being, and Hamm in the refuge does just that. It is interesting that this illusory power is reflected in formal terms in that there is a certain logical order in its expression, as if it were the only order possible in an incoherent universe. Witness for example Hamm's sadistic exchange with Clov (p. 20):

Hamm — Je ne te donnerai plus rien à manger.
Clov — Alors nous mourrons.
Hamm — Je te donnerai juste assez pour t'empêcher de
    mourir. Tu auras tout le temps faim.
Clov — Alors nous ne mourrons pas.

Suffering as negative experience is paralleled by a more general negation which runs as a leitmotif through both plays. Heidegger has defined very accurately, though in a different context, the point at which Beckett's writing has its source: 'It is the time of the gods that have fled and of the god that is coming. It is the time of need because it lies under a double Not: the No-more of the gods that have fled and the Not-yet of the god that is coming.'[4] This impasse-situation is expressible only in terms of void. It is first and foremost a situation of not-knowing: Vladimir and Estragon do not know when or even whether Godot will come — though we as the audience are bound by the play's internal logic to conclude that he will not. They do not know in any case what he will do for them even if he does come, living merely in the hope that he will somehow change their condition. There is a profound anti-rational element in this play as in all Beckett's writing, a deep suspicion of rational solution, and a conviction of the intellect's capacity for deceiving itself into answers concerning the human condition. Beckett refuses resolutely any principle of explanation as being inadequate or illusory, preferring the anguishing uncertainty of not-knowing. The behaviour of Godot towards the two boys, the shepherd whom he beats and the goatherd whom he does not, becomes a kind of microcosmic pattern for the incomprehensible nature of life in general. There is no point in asking why one person should suffer and not another, since there is no answer to the question. And no nobility in this ignorance, either.

If life is non-apprehendable through the intellect, it is not only because of man's intellectual limitations, but by virtue of a radical incoherence in the universe itself. There is no necessary connection between events or phenomena, one cannot predict from past experience how things will be the next time. And this in spite of the endlessly cyclic nature of things. The past has already disappeared into the void, so that yesterday is strictly non-interpretable in terms of today's needs. 'Hier' is

---

[4] *Existence and Being*, trans. D. Scott and R. F. C. Hull, New York, 1949, quot. *30*, p. 26.

only definable in terms of 'un foutu bout de misère', as we have already seen. Vladimir and Estragon gain no insight into Pozzo and Lucky's passage, or the boy's arrival, from the fact that it has already happened. The hierarchy of events and values which is absolutely crucial to our attempts to understand the world is lacking to Beckett's characters. All happens with an unnerving regularity which is at the same time unpredictable, there is a principle of undifferentiation at work which successfully foils any attempt at evaluation. When Hamm asks what time it is, he gets only the reply 'la même que d'habitude' (p. 18). Anthony Cronin has ably expressed this lack of differentiation in relation to Beckett's novels:

> Anything that happens in [one of Beckett's novels] will be important only in the poetic sense of being inescapable, not in the sense of being interesting, either as a cause or a result. A moment in a Beckett novel may be agonising, but it is not critical. We do not tremble for the outcome (*33,* p. 97).

The fate of Beckett's characters is in fact never in the balance, they do not develop through crises into resolution as in classical tragedy. In fact in this kind of tragedy there is no 'action' to speak of at all. The action is already complete before the curtain goes up, and the dramatic performance is only repeating what has already been accomplished (see *37,* p. 63). Beckett's use of repetition, as in the two acts of *Godot* or, even more strikingly, in the straight repetition of *Comédie,* is only underlining a fact which is inherent in the tragic vision.

One of the clearest manifestations of void in both plays is of course the omnipresence of absence. In *Fin de partie* the gaping void stretches between the present existence of the characters and their hoped-for and unattainable death. Death is thus the great positive which would signify an end to the negative of existence. In this play at least, death does not seem to be seen as total extinction, but as final absorption of the differentiated self in undifferentiation. Hamm describes it variously as 'petit plein perdu dans le vide' (p. 53), where the self is clearly still distinguished from the nothingness surrounding it, or 'petit gravier au milieu de la steppe' (p. 54), where there is identification but not total fusion.

Absence in *Godot* is obviously central to its whole construction. Godot is the relief that can never come, as well as being the foundation of Vladimir and Estragon's existence. They are sustained entirely by a being whom they have never seen, about whom they know next to nothing, and whose very existence is dubious. Having no authentic existence themselves, they are forced to rely on a being who is only definable in terms of his negative attributes. It is noteworthy that the only references to God are likewise totally negative. Lucky for example tells of 'un Dieu personnel [...] hors du temps hors de l'étendue qui du haut de sa divine apathie sa divine athambie sa divine aphasie nous aime bien' (p. 59), while Hamm addresses his prayers to a non-existent God — but whose very non-existence seems to be his defining characteristic, thus giving it a kind of nightmarish reality. 'Le salaud. Il n'existe pas' (p. 76), he says, when he realises there is no response to his prayers, taking Vigny's rejection of an uncommunicating God in the *envoi* to 'Le Mont des Oliviers' one step further, parodying his stoicism. When Clov picks this up with his mysterious 'Pas encore' — incidentally almost the only time in a world that is running down that something is mentioned in future terms — it seems to reinforce the affinity with Heidegger's comment in the passage quoted above on ours being the time of 'the Not-yet of the god that is coming'.

In this atmosphere of total negativity even guilt, that negative experience that is normally destined to impel us into something positive, repentance or expiation, has a negative, despairing quality. As we have seen, the crime of which man is guilty, the crime of being born, is precisely that for which he cannot be held responsible. This in fact is true of the tragic consciousness in general: the sin for which the hero is being punished is always involuntary and unavoidable, the punishment always far beyond what is strictly just in human terms, when any notion of individual responsibility is considered. As Beckett puts it:

> Tragedy is the statement of an expiation, but not the
> miserable expiation of a codified breach of a local
> arrangement organised by the knaves for the fools. The
> tragic figure represents the expiation of original sin, of
> the original and eternal sin of him and all his *socii
> malorum,* the sin of having been born (*10,* p. 67).

Because such guilt is linked to the fact of existence itself,
rather than to any supposed evil-doing, it is a kind of pre-
moral and certainly pre-legal position: we are guilty in metaphysical rather than moral or judicial terms. Again the
principle of undifferentiation operates: if our crime is common
to all, then it becomes a matter of indifference how we act in
this life. Life itself is expiation, and how we conduct ourselves
is a matter of little importance. But at the same time, since
guilt is universal, it becomes generalised, so that our con-
sciences are — obscurely — uneasy about most of what we
do. Hamm defends himself feebly against Clov's charge that
he allowed la Mère Pegg to 'die of darkness', but in the end
tries to throw the responsibility for universal suffering
elsewhere: 'Mais réfléchissez, réfléchissez, vous êtes sur terre,
c'est sans remède!' (p. 91).

The most we can say of guilt in this situation is that it is a
kind of 'présence négative de Dieu', as Jean-Marie Domenach
puts it (*34,* p. 276), that if we can speak of tragedy at all in this
context it is by a kind of 'inversion des signes' (*34,* p. 277),
this type of theatre being the negative form of what constitutes
classical tragedy, taking its contours from traditional form, but
lacking the positive substance. That there is behind the refusal
to make any positive statement a nostalgia for the latter is
beyond doubt: all Beckett's characters look back implicitly or
explicitly to a mythical moment when life had meaning and
purpose, while recognising that such a moment is dead, if it
ever existed. But the yearning is there, and this nostalgia is
perhaps the nearest we can get to a positive statement in
Beckett. Peter Brook puts the point forcefully:

> Beckett does not say 'no' with satisfaction; he forges
> his merciless 'no' out of a longing for 'yes' and so his

despair is the negative from which the contour of its opposite can be drawn (*31, p. 65*).

If one could encapsulate in a single word the content of this nostalgia it would be: order. The negatives we have already considered — incoherence, irrationality, ignorance, un-differentiation — all these are reducible in their positive form to a sense of order. Order would impose a necessity upon life, furnish connections which would lend intelligibility to the universe, provide a means of understanding and rationally directing action. Clov's dream of order, when everything would be silent in its final resting-place (p. 78), although a projection towards the end of the universe, is in fact nothing but this desire for comprehension, for rationality, where the incoherent movement of life would be stilled. The same sentiments are expressed in *Malone meurt* (p. 53), where Sapo looks forward to the moment when 'tout serait silencieux et noir et les choses seraient à leur place pour toujours, enfin'. All Beckett's characters sustain an agony of ignorance, and feel betrayed in a situation they do not understand but which cries out for explanation. They have the human longing for coherence in a world which defies rationality. Sometimes the ultimate principle of explanation is apparently benign — though this is never certain — like Godot, sometimes it is potentially hostile, a kind of Kafkaesque figure or undefined collectivity, the mysterious 'they' referred to by Clov and the narrator of *L'Innommable,* who may one day consider their sins to have been expiated.

In the meantime the search for order manifests itself through language, the attempt *par excellence* to impose order on the chaos of existence, language which can differentiate, categorise, connect. But the attempt is doomed in advance, and the characters know this as they tell their stories and their jokes, fill in time endlessly with words, words, words. The tension towards explanation is always the same, as is Beckett's rigorous refusal to provide any, or even to accept the possibility of one. There is no hope — and yet our only hope is that there is no hope. Beckett's work is infused with a kind of

'pitié exterminatrice' (*37*, p. 23), a savage compassion that
excludes sympathy and consolation, that is painstakingly destructive not only of illusion but also of everything man has
ever lived by. If his vision is not a comfortable one, it is
because his role is not that of the moralist: he can teach us
not how to live, but how to see.

(In) Conclusion

'Et cependant j'hésite encore à [...] finir.'
(Fin de partie)

W HAT Beckett wishes us to see is evidently extremely bleak. In his implacable demolition of the human, there seems little cover for high ideals, any more than there is for wishful thinking or for the subterfuges constantly invented by all of us, however well-intentioned, to hide our nakedness. A 'poor, bare, forked animal', indeed. The greyness in the setting and tone of such a play as *Fin de partie* is only the physical realisation of a terrifying greyness in the universe at large, a conviction that colour may be illusory, misleading, and is therefore to be avoided. In a situation where nothing is known for certain, the only honest course of action is to avoid making positive statements, which are at their most dangerous when most attractive — when they could all too obviously be based on what we desire rather than what is. Not that Beckett denies the force of these desires: one of the basic tensions in his work springs precisely from this consciousness of the conflict between the world-as-it-is and the world-as-it-should-be. In fact few writers have equalled Beckett in the presentation of this conflict: *Fin de partie* is perhaps the most exquisitely controlled and sustained cry of pain at the human condition that our theatre has to offer. And yet, because of the uncompromising integrity with which Beckett puts forward his vision, there is something curiously exhilarating about the play, and Beckett's writing in general. To touch bottom is in the end strangely comforting.

Because of the absolute nature of the analysis, Beckett has found old forms to be inadequate. In his view, the task of the artist traditionally has been to impose order on chaos, to demonstrate salvation through art in the sense that artistic form creates an order that is apparently lacking in the universe as a whole. The artist reproduces in this way the original act of creation, if by creation we mean the ordering of disparate elements into a coherent whole. The *logos* of creation is the same as the word that distinguishes, codifies, gives form to that which has none. But for Beckett this task of the artist is no longer valid. The artist still has to search for the appropriate form, but it must be a form that takes account of the original chaos, rather than abolishing it. His comment on *Comment c'est* is revealing in this respect:

> What I am saying does not mean that there will henceforth be no form in art. It only means that there will be new form, and that this form will be of such a type that it admits the chaos, and does not try to say that the chaos is really something else. The form and the chaos remain separate. The latter is not reduced to the former. That is why the form itself becomes a preoccupation, because it exists as a problem separate from the material it accommodates. To find a form that accommodates the mess, that is the task of the artist now. [1]

Sometimes Beckett indeed gives the impression that it is *only* the form that matters, that all art is a kind of abstract painting, where formal considerations are the only ones that count, indeed the only relevant ones. I myself have tended to emphasise this point in the course of this study, in the interests of making clear Beckett's particular priorities. But the point should not be neglected that form is only successful insofar as it approximates to what is being said — notwithstanding Beckett's claim in the Duthuit dialogues that there is 'nothing to express'. Beckett's success in *Godot* and *Fin de partie* is indeed a formal one, but only because of the appro-

---

[1] Tom Driver, 'Beckett by the Madeleine', *Columbia University Forum,* IV, 3 (Summer 61), 21-25.

priateness of the form he has found. It is a form that does not seek to deny 'the mess' — much of the plays' impact is due to the agonised consciousness of 'the mess' that comes through to the audience — but attempts to transmit it in all its purity.

In this Beckett is a poet, writing a genuinely poetic theatre. His attitude to language is utterly poetic, in that he is not trying to put over a 'message' that could be summarised in terms other than those in which it is already couched. His use of language is non-discursive, it does not tell a story that has a beginning, a middle and an end, or put forward an argument that progresses stage by stage towards a conclusion. It is strictly non-historical, and this applies of course equally well to his attitude to time. Temporal progression in these plays, as we have seen, is either cyclic or non-existent. The characters come from nowhere, do not develop in any rationally explicable way, and go to nowhere in the end. They perceive time as incoherent, frequently terrifying, outside their comprehension. The poet's capacity for seizing reality in one instantaneous moment is amply demonstrated in the two plays.

But this is not poetry of the page. By using the theatre as the vehicle for transmitting his vision, Beckett has enriched his form immeasurably, sometimes indeed by imposing on it new necessities. For instance, the theatre has obliged Beckett to impose on his audience temporal necessities that never shackle the reader of a poem, but these temporal necessities are so much a part of what he is trying to say that the work gains enormously from this servitude. Poetry, by being absorbed into a temporal element, is given the inevitability, the ultimate necessity, of music.

By using the medium of the theatre, again, Beckett has given to his writing the additional dimension of presence, presence in action. To the language of words he has added the language of gesture, and has not only accepted but also exploited the counterpoint between the two. Unlike the characters in the novels, Beckett's theatre characters — at least in the early plays — do not just talk, they exist in a physical sense, and the inadequacy of their physical existence is again an essential part of what is being communicated.

Perhaps most of all because it is a form of poetry, the last word will never be said on Beckett's theatre. However rigorously we analyse, a fundamental and necessary ambiguity must remain, and give to the language a multivalence that does not apply to the language of ordinary communication. The critic can only react to the plays as honestly as he can, and give tentative pointers for a reading. In the end it is the public, the audiences who from that first performance of *Godot* in Paris in 1953 have reacted with enthusiasm, hostility, bemusement, recognition, that will make these plays continue to live. They belong so essentially to the world of the theatre, they teach us so much about the nature of theatre, in its total reliance on physical presence and suggestion, and its submission to time which all too briefly it also conquers, that any attempt to talk about them, especially on the printed page, is doomed to failure. The critic cannot make a play live: all he can do is help to create the conditions whereby the public will want to make it live, through the catalysing process of repeated performance.

Select Bibliography

I. EDITIONS OF PLAYS DISCUSSED

1 *En attendant Godot,* Paris: Edns de Minuit, 1952 (1976 printing).
2 *En attendant Godot,* ed. Colin Duckworth, London: George Harrap, 1966.
3 *Waiting for Godot,* London: Faber and Faber, 1956.
4 *Fin de partie, suivi de Acte sans paroles I,* Paris: Edns de Minuit, 1957.
5 *Fin de partie,* ed. John and Beryl Fletcher, London: Methuen, 1970.
6 *Endgame,* London: Faber and Faber, 1958.
N.B. *1* and *4* have now been collected in *Théâtre,* Vol. I, Paris: Edns de Minuit, 1971.

II. OTHER TEXTS BY BECKETT TO WHICH SUBSTANTIAL REFERENCE IS MADE

7 *L'Innommable,* Paris: Edns de Minuit, 1953.
8 *Malone meurt,* Paris: Edns de Minuit, 1951.
9 *Mercier et Camier,* Paris: Union Générale d'Editions, Coll. 10/18, 1970.
10 *Proust and three dialogues,* London: Calder, 1966.

III. CRITICISM ON 'EN ATTENDANT GODOT' AND 'FIN DE PARTIE'

11 Cohn, Ruby, ed., *Casebook on Waiting for Godot,* New York: Grove Press Inc., 1967.
12 Lalande, Bernard, *'En attendant Godot': Beckett,* Paris: Hatier, Coll. Profil d'une œuvre, 1970.
13 Lavielle, Emile, *'En attendant Godot' de Beckett,* Paris: Hachette, Coll. Poche Critique, 1972.
14 States, Bert O., *The Shape of Paradox: an essay on 'Waiting for Godot',* Berkeley and Los Angeles: University of California Press, 1978.

15 Chevigny, Bell Gale, ed., *Twentieth Century Interpretations of 'Endgame'*, Englewood Cliffs, N.J.: Prentice-Hall Inc., 1969.

16 Wolf, Daniel & Edwin Fancher, ed., 'Beckett's letters on *Endgame'*, *The Village Voice Reader*, Garden City, New York: Grove Press, 1963.

IV. GENERAL CRITICISM ON BECKETT

17 Admussen, Richard L., *The Samuel Beckett Manuscripts: a study*, London: George Prior Publishers, 1979.

18 Bair, Deirdre, *Samuel Beckett*, London: Jonathan Cape, 1978.

19 Bishop, Tom, & R. Federman, ed., *Cahiers de l'Herne: Samuel Beckett*, Paris: L'Herne, 1976.

20 *Cahiers de la Compagnie Madeleine Renaud — Jean-Louis Barrault* (Paris, Julliard), no. 44 (Oct. 63).

21 Coe, Richard, *Beckett*, London: Oliver & Boyd Ltd, revised edn 1968.

22 Cohn, Ruby, *Back to Beckett*, Princeton, N.J.: Princeton U.P., 1973.

23 ———, *Samuel Beckett: the comic gamut*, New Brunswick, N.J.: Rutgers U.P., 1962.

24 Graver, L. & R. Federman, ed., *The Critical Heritage: Samuel Beckett*, London: Routledge & Kegan Paul, 1979.

25 Janvier, Ludovic, *Beckett par lui-même*, Paris: Edns du Seuil, Coll. Ecrivains de toujours, 1969.

26 ———, *Pour Samuel Beckett*, Paris: Union Générale d'Editions, Coll. 10/18, 1966.

27 *Modern Drama*, IX (1966) [special number Samuel Beckett].

28 Nores, Dominique, ed., *Les Critiques de notre temps et Beckett*, Paris: Edns Garnier, 1971.

29 Reid, Alec, *All I Can Manage, More Than I Could: an approach to the plays of Samuel Beckett*, Dublin: Dolmen Press, 1968.

30 Robinson, Michael, *The Long Sonata of the Dead*, London: Hart-Davis, 1969.

V. GENERAL WORKS

31 Brook, Peter, *The Empty Space*, Harmondsworth: Penguin Books, 1968.

32 Brunel, Pierre, ed., *La Mort de Godot. Attente et évanescence au théâtre. Albee, Beckett, Betti et al. Essais réunis et présentés par Pierre Brunel*, Paris: Minard, Coll. Situations, no. 23, 1970.

33 Cronin, Anthony, *A Question of Modernity*, London: Secker & Warburg, 1966.

34 Domenach, Jean-Marie, *Le Retour du tragique*, Paris: Edns du Seuil, 1967.

35 Esslin, Martin, *The Theatre of the Absurd*, Harmondsworth: Penguin Books, revised and enlarged edn 1968.

36 Kott, Jan, *Shakespeare our Contemporary*, London: Methuen, 1965.

37 Rosset, Clément, *La Logique du pire*, Paris: P.U.F., 1971.

38 Serreau, Geneviève, *Histoire du 'nouveau théâtre'*, Paris: Gallimard, Coll. Idées, 1966.

The reader is also referred in a general way to the valuable *Journal of Beckett Studies*, published by the University of Reading twice yearly, January 1977 onwards.